MISSION-DRIVEN LEADERSHIP

MISSION-DRIVEN LEADERSHIP

My Journey as a Radical Capitalist

MARK BERTOLINI

CURRENCY

NEW YORK

All rights reserved.
Published in the United States by Currency, an imprint of the Crown Publishing Group, a division of Penguin Random House LLC, New York.
currencybooks.com

CURRENCY and its colophon are trademarks of Penguin Random House LLC.

Currency books are available at special discounts for bulk purchases for sales promotions or corporate use. Special editions, including personalized covers, excerpts of existing books, or books with corporate logos, can be created in large quantities for special needs. For more information, contact Premium Sales at (212) 572-2232 or e-mail specialmarkets@penguinrandomhouse.com.

Library of Congress Cataloging-in-Publication Data

Names: Bertolini, Mark
Title: Mission-driven leadership : my journey as a radical capitalist / Mark Bertolini.
Description: New York : Currency, [2019] | Includes index.
Identifiers: LCCN 2018040717 | ISBN 9780525572794
Subjects: LCSH: Bertolini, Mark | Insurance executives—United States—Biography. | Chief executive officers—United States—Biography. | Leadership. | Insurance companies—United States—Management. | Health insurance—United States
Classification: LCC HG8042.B44 A3 2019 | DDC 658.4/092—dc23 LC record available at https://lccn.loc.gov/2018040717

ISBN 978-0-525-57279-4
Ebook ISBN 978-0-525-57280-0

Printed in the United States of America

Jacket design by Luis Heinrich
Jacket photograph by Emma McIntyre/Getty Images

10 9 8 7 6 5 4 3 2 1

First Edition

NOTHING GREAT HAPPENS WITHOUT FAMILY:

To Mari . . .
your love of all things opens my eyes to a more beautiful world . . .
your joyful light chases out the darkness inside me . . .

To Lauren . . .
the love of a daughter is one of life's greatest gifts . . .
walking hand-in-hand together along life's way is a joy that can
never be fully expressed . . .

To Eric . . .
your courageous journey is my life's greatest learning . . .
your happiness as a man, husband, and father is your greatest gift.

Contents

Prologue

VECTORING THROUGH THE STORM

ALL CORPORATE LEADERS TRAVEL A LONG ROAD TO THE top, but once they arrive, they discover that nothing they've done has truly prepared them. So, their instinct is to be restrained, cautious: I've got all this power. I've got all these responsibilities. I've got all these people—employees, customers, shareholders—who now depend on me.

My main purpose is, don't screw it up.

Such is the weight of any leadership position. I felt it when I was named the chief executive officer of the Aetna Corporation in 2010. Much earlier in my career, I had been the CEO of a small health maintenance organization, and I had held senior positions at several large insurers. But I would now be leading a Fortune 100 company that served more than 35 million people across the globe, had $34 billion in revenue, and would soon be paying for health care in every country around the world. Aetna is an industry pillar with a distinguished history, having survived two world wars and the Great Depression as well as the Civil War. Founded in 1853, it wrote life insurance policies for Union soldiers worried about their dependents. It paid claims from the Chicago fire in 1871 and from the San Francisco earthquake in 1906, and it wrote life insurance policies for NASA's first astronauts. In one of our darker chapters, Aetna also issued reparation policies to slave owners, who were then paid back when one of their slaves ran away.

My initial conversations with board members did not put me at ease. The directors told me they felt fortunate that I would be the next person running the company, but there was one catch. Given the increased concerns over the compensation of CEOs, I would not be receiving much of a raise. That was surprising, and I needed to think about it. Betsy Cohen was head of the compensation committee, and I soon met with her at her place in Maine, overlooking the Atlantic. We were on the beach, the water lapping at our feet, a bottle of wine at the ready.

I told her, "I think I can do this if you honor your commitment that if I do the right thing over the next three years, you'll reward me for it."

Betsy was a lawyer by training who had founded two different banks in Philadelphia over a long, trailblazing career. She considered my request and nodded.

We clinked glasses and I asked, "We're done, then?"

Not quite.

"You know," she said, "if you mess it up, we'll shoot you in the head."

And she smiled at me.

(Betsy proved to be a brilliant mentor and trusted advisor.)

The playful threat was a reminder that I would now be held accountable in completely new ways, and the board, I'm sure, had its own concerns. Its members already knew that I was unconventional. Yes, I was driven and demanding, but I also had a radical streak, particularly for a conservative company like Aetna. I practice yoga and meditation and, as Aetna's president, offered those activities to our employees as a workplace benefit. I have half a dozen tattoos, wear old jeans to the office, and generally don't look like your typical corporate chieftain. I told the board that as CEO, I was not going to always wear a tie to work, and I wasn't going to always shave. I would use social media to communicate directly with our members (or customers), and even though I have a disabled left arm, I would continue to downhill-ski and ride my motorcycle.

Why? Because that's who I am, and I need to be me if I'm going to do this job.

THIS BOOK IS my attempt to explain some of the skills and insights that I believe are essential for any leader in America today, a book that draws heavily on my own experiences—the good, the bad, and the near fatal. If you work in the business world, you already know about our challenges with global economic change and technological disruptions, and how those have changed the leader's role. The days are long gone when CEOs, or anyone in power, can dictate the truth to those they seek to lead. Our employees now receive their information from supercomputers in their pockets, rendering edicts from the mount (or the C-suite) as just another item in their already crowded newsfeed. We still run businesses out of brick or glass buildings, but the four walls don't exist as they used to: employees now have instant access to what's happening at other companies across their city, across their country, and even across the world. They are emboldened, smart, and skeptical. If you say something that isn't true, they will correct you; if you do something that's misguided, they will expose you; and if you fear the moment, they will challenge, ridicule, or ignore you.

Authority isn't what it used to be.

I have other concerns. When I became CEO, I told the board that one of my goals was to restore the credibility of corporate leadership in the eyes of Americans. That credibility has eroded, I believe, because of our own passivity in the face of dire social problems. Corporations can't be run like medieval city-states against the plague, with the drawbridge raised and everyone hiding behind the castle walls. The plague isn't going away, and our politicians seem paralyzed, so companies have to take the lead on such problems as income inequality, education, and health care.

I admit to being an unlikely voice of the establishment. I grew up railing against "the man." Which is fine, except then one day I became "the man," so now what? The answer is, to share what I've discovered, about leadership and life, in a way that will be meaningful to others.

What I have to share also reflects a personal journey that I wouldn't wish on anyone but which brought me to where I am today.

I grew up in Detroit, part of a large, blue-collar family, and I had expectations of doing better than my father, with enough money for a place in northern Michigan where I could go on the weekends, riding snowmobiles in the winter, hunting in the fall, and shooting pool year-round. Almost as an afterthought, I got an MBA and embarked on a career in health care management. My main skill is that I know how to fix things, and I've held a series of jobs that have required me to either start up or turn around a business.

That trajectory, culminating in my becoming Aetna's CEO and then chairman, is not dissimilar to that of many executives. What is different is that I experienced two traumatic events in my personal life that changed me as a person and a leader. My son, Eric, as a teenager, was diagnosed with an incurable cancer—an ordeal, in its physical and emotional toll, that no family should endure—and the experience forced me to rethink my values and priorities in life, not to mention our country's entire approach to health care. I was then in a ski accident in Vermont; I broke five vertebrae, cracked my scapula, avulsed my nerve roots, and was left unconscious in a frozen creek. My last rites were read while I lay in a coma in a New Hampshire hospital bed. After six days, I woke up, but I now had a disabled left arm that throbbed with pain and that is beyond the care of Western medicine.

My injuries changed me in many ways, as I had to reinvent how I did the most basic tasks (I now use my teeth to open a bag of chips). I also had to accept that some of my favorite activities (running, lifting weights, playing a piano) were forever out of reach. The personal impact, however, was only part of it. I also had to ask myself a hard question: was I really devoting my career to anything that was meaningful?

If I was going to continue working; if I was going to continue to push myself and the people around me to reach new heights; if I was going to continue to sacrifice time with family and friends to assume the obligations of leading a company, then I needed to be on a mission.

Thus began, for me, the idea of mission-driven leadership.

Leadership is all about followership, and people will follow you if they embrace the mission. That mission is about charting a path that everyone can follow, even during times of turbulence (and those times are inevitable). I call this "vectoring through the storm." When the ship is thrown off course and the gales are howling, the crew wants to know that the captain is on deck, clenching the tiller, not lounging in the cabin drinking Madeira.

Each of us is on our own life journey, and for me that

journey has made me a better person and a better leader. As a corporate executive, I had to move beyond the balance sheet and the financials, and I sought a broader perspective that redefined the values of our organization and identified ways to make a real difference in people's lives. I had to become less righteous and more empathetic. I needed to dictate less and listen more. I needed to learn. I needed to connect. I also had to lose attachments—to ideas that proved outdated, to a self-image that no longer existed, and to corporate models that no longer worked.

Ultimately, I had to lose the very company that I led.

All of these efforts did indeed drive significant bottom-line success for Aetna, and I eventually got my raise. But the greatest rewards have been in what we actually accomplished: defying norms to create a better workplace, designing a new approach for engagement with the community, and reimagining our mission to build a healthier world.

That style of leadership is a lot more noble than *don't screw it up.* It's more fun as well.

1

DOING THE RIGHT THING

"DO THINGS RIGHT" IS A CORE VALUE, SEEMINGLY BE-yond reproach as a corporate motto. When you're at your job—either on the front lines or in a corner office—you do things right, or else you'll fail.

But what if that truism isn't true at all? Do things right usually means "follow the rules." But what if the rules are flawed, suboptimal, or counterproductive? Most of us have a moral compass that allows us to distinguish between right and wrong. What's trickier, however, is distinguishing between doing things right and *doing the right thing.* You can be follow-ing the rules but still be betraying your mission or your values.

This may seem like a subtle distinction, but understanding it sets apart those who want to make positive change from those who just want to reinforce the status quo. It's a lesson I've learned many times in my life.

When I was attending college in the late 1970s, I worked evening shifts in the emergency room at St. John Hospital and Medical Center in Detroit. I was the department coordina-tor, which meant I sat at the front desk and performed tri-age, deciding who among our incoming wounded or stricken was most in need of immediate attention. The ER was also a Level I trauma center, one of the busiest in the nation, a place that was turbulent, tragic, and exhilarating all at once. I liked being part of the action.

At least once a night a patient arrived who'd had a heart attack, and sometimes I would jump on the gurney to relieve the EMT guys. I'd have a Marlboro in my mouth, the ashes falling on the patient as I was doing compressions. That was perfectly acceptable back then. As we approached the oxygen room, I'd yell, "Take it out of my mouth!" since a cigarette—amid the flammable anesthesia—could blow up the place. Someone would snatch the Marlboro just before we entered.

We once admitted a woman who'd had a heart attack but was also suffering from lung cancer. I was doing compressions but could feel her bones crack because the cancer was so advanced. I yelled to the doctor, "I'm crushing her ribs!" He told the nurse to give her twenty milligrams of Demerol and administer it "PRN"—as needed—until she passed away.

Euthanasia. Happened all the time.

On another occasion, a buddy's father was rushed in while he was having a heart attack. I did compressions on him, urging him to hang on. After he was taken to a cardiac room, he was intubated while others worked on him. I came in and out of the room, relaying information about his medical history, gleaned from his family, while he lay unconscious. He survived and was sent to the coronary care unit. Three weeks later, after he was discharged, he walked into the ER and informed me that he had heard everything I was saying while he was unconscious. "It was like I was sitting in the corner of the room, up in the air," he explained. "I could hear everything you said."

Working in the ER was about life and death as well as the occasional out-of-body experience, but it was also about how we assign different value to human life, based on wealth, influence, or privilege. Our failure to treat all people as equals was casual and easily accepted, and it left a powerful mark.

One night I was at the front the desk when a young man,

lying on a gurney, was hustled through our sliding doors. Shot twice by a .22-caliber handgun, he was bleeding from his ear but had no exit wounds. He didn't have his wallet; we didn't know his name. But we saw, in his X-ray, his fate: the image showed the bullets lodged in his brain, like two white islands in a sea of gray.

The doctors spent forty-five minutes evaluating him, but the victim was dead on arrival, another nameless casualty of Detroit's mean streets. The doctors had no other option but to send him to our morgue.

Later in the evening, the police arrived with the victim's wallet. He had been a college student who also worked as a cabdriver, and he had been murdered on the job while getting robbed. Now that we knew who he was, it was my responsibility to notify his parents.

I called the number and identified myself.

"What are you bothering me for?" the man said. "I'm not on call."

"Who is this?" I asked.

He told me who he was, a senior doctor at St. John Hospital.

"Your son is in the ER," I said. "He's had an accident, and you need to come down here."

"What happened?"

"You need to come down here."

When I hung up, I informed the staff who the victim's father was and that he would be here shortly to identify his son. It was like an alarm sounded. Assistants scurried to the morgue and retrieved the body, and the doctors spent another half hour trying to revive him—to raise him from the dead, literally. When that failed, they cleaned the wound to make the body more presentable to the father.

Even in death, status had its privileges.

I eventually realized that we operated based on an unwritten social hierarchy, and we allocated our resources accordingly. Those who had money and influence received preferred treatment while everyone else waited in line. That was, in this ER, *doing things the right way,* according to custom, consistent with expectations. I couldn't change anything. I was too junior. But I found ways to convey my opposition.

The ER was typically overcrowded, often due to the neglect of those who worked in the system. A patient would notify his doctor of an urgent medical problem, but the doctor, either out of laziness or lack of capacity, would not want to admit him until morning, so that patient came to the emergency room. Other patients who lacked clout or connections showed up because they had no other place to go. But we had no available beds, so we became a holding station of last resort. Sometimes we'd have thirty patients lying on gurneys in the hallway. I called them "patients under the clock." They were often drug users, homeless people, misfits; the disadvantaged and the dispossessed. Some had chest pains; others had broken hips; others, we weren't even sure. The hospital had the room and the resources, on the floors above, to care for these individuals, but it wasn't a priority. So there they lay, all night, under the clock.

One night I took their names and made out a "VIP Notification List," and then slid that list under the door of the hospital CEO so that he would see it first thing in the morning.

I wanted him to know that these were the people—VIPs all—whom we failed to serve the night before in the emergency room.

My insubordination could have gotten me into trouble, but it was the right thing to do.

That kind of attitude has led me to take some defiant stands in the workplace, but it has also helped me realize many of my goals. My colleagues may not always agree with me, but I believe they know that I'm driven to do the right thing, particularly in those instances when I've upset conventional wisdom or challenged powerful interests.

I also fight for what I believe in, which came from my youth. I grew up in a family and a community that, one way or another, was always under the clock.

I WAS BORN in Detroit in 1956, the oldest of six children born seven years apart. Think Italian and Irish Catholic as well as biblical. My mother named the four boys after three apostles (John, Peter, and Philip) and a gospel (Mark). My father named the girls Angela and Nina. We lived for several years on the East Side, in a neighborhood that no longer exists, and then our growing family moved to the outskirts of the city, to St. Clair Shores. If our country was in the midst of a great postwar boom, I certainly wasn't aware of it. My father was a tenuously employed pattern maker in the auto industry, and my mother worked once a week at a pediatrician's office so she could bring home the vaccines. Our one-thousand-square-foot house had one bathroom, and we were allowed one bath a week. The kids were left scrambling for food, clothes, and attention. When we sat down for dinner, we had a Lazy Susan, and once you took your portion, that was all you got. Each school year, I'd get a pair of Kmart tennis shoes, a pair of pants, and three shirts, and if I wanted them clean, I'd wash and iron them myself. (Our ironing board was attached to a wall in the kitchen.) I slept in a bunk with my brother Phil, and our sisters had to walk through our room to get to theirs. During the winter, when the backyards along our block froze into one long hockey rink, my brothers and I wrapped Sears catalogs around our legs and used them as shin guards.

My siblings and I were tight, always looking out for one another, which is what you'd expect in a family with strong Italian roots.

My paternal grandparents, who came to America in 1929, were pure and proud northern Italians—from the Tuscany region and Milan, with deep biases against other parts of the country. My wife's father was from the tip of the boot, and when we married in 1979, my paternal grandparents refused to attend the wedding.

My dad was a skilled carpenter, capable of making tables and chairs in our basement, but also, as a pattern maker, he created mahogany models to build car parts. The jobs were plentiful but never steady, so he'd bowl for extra income. After league games ended at 11 p.m., the after-hours competition began. They'd line up the pins, pay five bucks a game, and play until 5 a.m. The top winner got 60 percent of the pot, and if you had a hot hand, you'd do pretty well. I also played and entered tournaments and became quite good. My dad wanted me to be a professional bowler. That didn't happen, but my bowling income did help me pay for college.

My mom's parents worked as the nanny and chauffeur for the Remick family in nearby Grosse Point (Jerome Remick was a famous music publisher), so my mother grew up in the servant quarters of a ten-thousand-square-foot mansion with nine bedrooms, twelve bathrooms, and an indoor pool. Her marriage to my dad was her ticket from abundance to scarcity.

As a nurse, she had a career outside the home, but she was soon trapped in a succession of pregnancies. She regretted her decision to marry for the rest of her life, and to vent her displeasure, she'd smack us for trivial sins or nag our dad to take out his belt and whip us. Our parents were not much different from most of the parents in our neighborhood. It was a different era, and the adults, toughened by the Great Depression and now struggling just to get by, ruled with an iron fist and little patience. My own parents never truly hurt us physically, and the verbal lashings were probably worse. My brothers and I used to joke that our names were "Ball Scratchin' Sons of Bitches." My mom once told Angela that if she had to do it over again, she would have stopped after three children. Angela was the fourth.

My father had a competitive streak that he made sure he passed on to his kids. When my brothers and I fought in the house, he'd take us outside, and sitting at a picnic table, he'd take a long drag on his Lucky Strike, drop the ashes into the cuff of his pants, and say, "The two of you will now fight until one of you gives up." And that's what we'd do.

My dad also brooked no dissent. One time he was working in the garage and told me to take out the garbage. I said I had to play ball. "I want it taken out now," he said. But I kept on walking. And then—*whap!*—a hammer sailed right past my head and stuck in the wall. I turned and looked at him, and he was glaring at me. "It will be in the middle of your head the next time," he said. "Take the garbage out."

That's how we grew up. Life's a struggle. Don't expect any breaks. Only the toughest survive. On weekend mornings, we'd walk to the ball field and choose teams. No one received participation awards or was even guaranteed to play. If you weren't chosen, you'd sit on the bench and watch the entire game. You were considered a loser and were expected to practice until you were good enough to get picked. It was a Darwinian world, and it etched a combative streak within me that I carried for the rest of my life.

Even in this environment, our struggles were often attached to a larger moral code, which my father enforced in his own distinctive way.

I began working for my dad when I was thirteen, and when I was at South Lake High School, I'd finish my classes at 1 p.m. and take a bus over to a large pattern-making shop, where my dad was foreman. I'd sweep the floors, paint, take care of the lawn. A guy named Jerry was doing the same work, and one day we were having a cigarette, and he mentioned that he was making four dollars an hour.

I was making a lot less, so I went to my dad.

"Jerry's making four dollars an hour," I said. "I'm making a dollar twenty-five. I want a raise."

"What are you going to do if I don't give you one?" he asked.

"I'm going to quit," I said.

"Oh, really? Do you have another job?"

"No."

"Great. You're fired. Go home."

So, I went home, and that evening, we had family dinner, in which my dad, as always, held court on current events. After dinner, he told me to stay at the table.

"So how does it feel to be unemployed?" he asked.

"Not good," I said.

"Let me tell you about Jerry. He's twenty-eight years old. He's not very smart. As a matter of fact, he's mentally challenged, and this is the only work he'll ever be able to do. And he's got a wife and a son. And I'm supporting him and his family. You're fifteen years old. You're going to go to college. You're going to do good things. You're getting spending money. So, I shouldn't be paying you the same I'm paying Jerry, because Jerry is never going to be anything more than what he is right now."

"Yeah," I said. "I guess I understand."

"Do you want to come back to work?"

"Yeah."

"Okay. A buck an hour."

He cut my pay.

It was a typical lesson from my father—don't challenge his authority—but also a lesson, as he saw it, in helping someone who had a disability.

The Vietnam War was another battlefield in our house. I was nine when the United States began its first major escalation, and the conflict dragged on as I approached the draft age. I had an older cousin, Jimmy, who served there, and he sent me a Viet Cong military field jacket that a soldier had been wearing when Jimmy killed him. Bullet holes riddled the jacket, and Jimmy had bleached out the bloodstains. My brother and I wore it to school, proudly, but I didn't have any illusions about the war.

That was the backdrop when in 1973 I received my draft card–1A, to be exact, my lottery number thirty-seven. My mom wanted me to go to college and become a doctor, and when I showed her my draft card, she said, "Oh my God, you're going to get killed in Vietnam!"

She told me I would go to Canada, but my father, a Korean War vet, thought draft dodgers represented everything that was wrong with America. That night at dinner, a huge argument erupted between my parents about whether I should go to Canada or Vietnam, until I finally said, "Hold on. This is my life, and I'll decide what I'm going to do."

The next thing I knew, I was flat on my back, my dad

having smacked me across the mouth. "You're not going to be a pussy," he said. "You're going to war."

The draft ended before my number was called, but I would have gone. It would have been the right thing to do.

I didn't resent my parents. I felt sorry for them. They didn't understand birth control and had all these kids they didn't want, and I knew that their anger was not really directed at us. I also didn't need a great deal of direction to find my way, or so I thought.

I was the first kid in our family to attend college, Wayne State University in Detroit, but, lacking motivation and drinking too much beer, I flunked out after two years with a 1.79 grade point average. That put me on a different path, temporarily, that allowed me to see the world in a different way.

Between those who have power and those who don't.

Between those who follow the rules and those who defy them.

I got a job as an orderly in a nursing home, where we had a nurse who on occasion appeared addled. She had blond hair, a glass eye, and a limp, and I noticed that when she administered Demerol to patients, she did not give the whole amount but took some of it herself. One day, she was sitting in the cafeteria across from me. Her eyes rolled back, and she face-planted right into her slice of watermelon. When she looked up, a black seed was attached to her glass eye. She was so stoned, she didn't even know it.

I called the state police. They arrested her and told me that I had done good work. The police later called me and said they were investigating another nurse suspected of taking drugs, and they asked me to keep an eye on her. I did, and she too was arrested.

I didn't set out to be a police informant, but as far as I was concerned, if you put your drug habit ahead of your patients, you deserved to be turned in.

My informant role notwithstanding, I was also an outspoken advocate for the nursing home employees. The hours were long, the job hard; but what really bothered me were the low wages. The employees needed to organize, so I led the effort in trying to convince them to join the Services Employees International Union. I wasn't doing it for myself. I knew I'd be returning to college. I just thought that the employees were not receiving what they were due, and I was going to fight the manager with all my strength on their behalf.

Problem was, the manager was my mother.

After her kids were in school, my mom went back to college and got her bachelor of science in nursing, and she was hired by a nursing home four blocks from our house. She learned the business, and when the director of nursing retired, she got that job, and she hired me as well as other family members. Of course, when she hired me, she didn't anticipate my becoming a union organizer, which she saw as an act of rank betrayal.

Still and all, I was surprised by her response.

She fired me.

I knew that was against the law, and I told her. "I could call the Department of Labor, and you'd be in deep shit," I said.

She glared at me. "If they could ever find you."

So, I lost my job, my mom was never investigated, and the employees voted against the union. A clean-sweep defeat, but I still thought it was the right thing to do, and I continued that pattern—righteously speaking out—at my next job, at a Ford plant.

This time I was doing rear-axle differential-housing assembly on the Mercury Bobcat. I was working eighty-hour weeks; if I worked more than eight hours on a weekday, I received time and a half, and I got double time on Saturdays and triple time on Sundays. This was 1976, and I was making $60,000 a year, pretty good money back then, and I could have stayed there for years. But if I think something is broke or not performing well, I want to repair it. One day in the plant, it occurred to me that the workflow was inefficient—we had two people doing a job that could be handled by one. So, my buddy and I changed the assembly process, and that meant one guy did the work while the other guy took an hour break outside. This meant defying the rules, but the process was now more efficient (and it didn't hurt that we had outside a twelve-pack, some cigarettes, and a few magazines to pass the time).

At some point, the union steward came by. "What are you doing?" he asked me. "Where's your buddy?"

"He's outside," I said.

"What's going on here?"

"It's easier to do it this way."

"You can't redesign the workflow," he said. "It's very specific. The union negotiates it. Stop this shit, or you're going to cost us a job."

I was standing there with my heavy boots on, jeans, a sweatshirt, coveralls, goggles, and earplugs; a cigarette hung from my mouth, and I was covered in grease. And he was wearing khakis, a white dress shirt, and a red tie. I looked at him and said, "You know what, I'm the guy who actually improved this process, and you're telling me I can't do it, and you're standing there all clean in your white shirt. How do I get your job?"

"You got to have a degree," he said.

I went home, opened the Wayne State course book, and circled the classes I had already passed. I then put a square around the classes I had previously taken and had failed but could easily pass if I paid attention. I then determined what degree I could get in the shortest amount of time.

My 1.79 grade point average and I returned to Wayne State, where my brother John already played football. He later told others, "I'm so proud of my brother Mark. When I started at Wayne State, he was a sophomore, and when I graduated from Wayne State, he was a sophomore." I prefer to say that the eight years it took to get my degree showed my commitment.

THOSE EARLY WORK experiences taught me that right and wrong are often in competition with each other, and even when you do things right, you may be doing things wrong. As I attained more authority in my own career, I could do more than just agitate for change; I could make it myself. That is, in fact, one of the obligations of a leader—to reach down into the depths of an organization and set clear markers on what constitutes doing the right thing.

Aetna, for example, employs a fair number of doctors to help us assess therapies and determine coverage, but sometimes when they join us, they forget their mission as doctors. I once received an email from a new member who had hypertension. He explained that the drug that was covered by his previous insurer wasn't on our formulary, so Aetna was now requiring him to use "step therapy," or to try less expensive drugs, before we would cover the drug that he had been on. But the man said that he had other medical issues, and he sent a file that showed a chart, on page eight, indicating that he had optic nerve damage.

The guy was right. Given the seriousness of his medical condition, he should not be going on step therapy.

I picked up the phone and called our doctor who was in charge of the case.

"Why would you want to mess with someone's blood pressure who's got optic nerve damage?" I asked. "Do we want to blind him?"

The doctor said he thought that requiring step therapy was consistent with our policy. He was just following the rules.

"What's your job here?" I asked. "It's to make sure we don't hurt anybody and to ensure that everyone gets the right medical care. Use your head. You're a doctor. You had an obligation to look at this person's entire chart and approve the drug."

It was a classic example of someone who thought he was doing things right but did not take that extra step to do the right thing. What is it about our humanity that we bring to work each day? It's the ability to recognize the needs of others and to find ways to reduce their suffering, to offer comfort, and to treat people well. Sometimes you have to ignore the rules to do that and get to page eight.

Bold initiatives require flawless execution, but I've also learned that getting the little things right is just as important. They have a cumulative effect and can serve as building blocks for more ambitious projects. They can also set a tone for the values of the organization.

We introduced an Employee Awards Dinner at Aetna, in which we recognize outstanding frontline contributors and give them a bonus. The event is at our headquarters, so out-of-town employees travel to Hartford and visit me in my office, and it's just a meaningful way to show our employees how much we value them. The dinner itself, with all kinds of presentations, cheering, and laughter, reminds me of a corporate prom. Everyone is happy to be there. Names are called out, and I greet each winner onstage, where I give that person a hug, and we have our picture taken. At one of these dinners, a winner was a military veteran who'd been at Aetna for several years and was recognized for his outstanding work at the company. I took my picture with him, and he was beaming from ear to ear. It was a wonderful moment.

Two months later came the devastating news: he committed suicide. Suicide rates among our military veterans is an underreported crisis. In the case of our employee, we knew that he had struggled with addiction, but we thought those issues were behind him, and we proudly hired him as part of our commitment to give our veterans a chance to reenter the workforce. None of us knew the deeper pain that he was still in. (I now assume that he had PTSD.)

Three or four weeks after he died, I received a letter from his parents, with the very photo of him and me, my arm around him, taken at the awards dinner. According to his parents, the photo had been on his desk in his room.

"Thank you so much for giving my son a chance," they wrote. "This was the proudest day of his life."

I hope that picture, in capturing a moment of joy, brought a ray of comfort to the parents. For me, it was a reminder that the smallest of gestures can have a meaningful impact. You never know when doing the right thing can be the proudest moment in a person's life.

1

THE FALSE GODS OF EXCEL

NUMBERS HAVE ALWAYS FASCINATED ME. I WAS A MATH prodigy as a kid, as I found clarity and precision in that world and enjoyed the challenge of solving complex problems. In college, I learned how to do probability-weighted-average-net-present-value calculations and net-probability-distribution cash flows. I also learned how to count cards at casinos.

Corporate America loves numbers because they make life easy to track and measure, and I certainly use data in my presentations to prove my points and support my arguments. But charts, graphs, and stats can also be used to distort the truth, to divert attention, to obscure the larger mission of the organization. Numbers are objective; not so the people who use them.

I learned long ago that to find out what's behind the numbers, you have to dig deeper, and sometimes you have to go out and see it for yourself.

In 1994, after I was hired by the New York Life Insurance Company, I took a walk through the mailroom. Back then, mailrooms were large, chaotic portals through which companies interacted with the outside world, and I noticed that our large machine to open letters stood silent while we had four guys sitting at a table with letter openers. They were doing the same thing the machine was supposed to do, except it took them longer, and we were paying four guys to do it.

I asked one of the supervisors what was going on.

He told me the blade on the letter-opening machine was broken, so they hired four workers to open the mail.

"Why don't you just get a new blade?" I asked.

He said a new blade cost $700, but the letter openers only cost $40 apiece.

"Sure, but what about the four guys you're paying?"

He told me it was the manager's decision.

So I walked into the manager's office, and he was sitting with his feet up on a massive desk, three-quarters of which was covered with giveaways from vendors, and a large ink blotter in the middle.

"This is crazy," I told him. "You've got four people opening the mail. Why don't you just buy a new blade?"

He told me I didn't understand the math. The blade would cost $700, but the four letter openers only cost $160. "We're saving $540," he told me.

"But what about the people!"

He calmly explained that his "people budget" wasn't as tight as his "supply budget," so it "actually makes more sense to do it this way."

Well, we soon got a new machine blade, not to mention a new mailroom manager, and the incident spoke volumes about how some businesses are run. The mailroom manager would have been given high marks for staying within his budget. He hit his numbers! And the numbers took priority over what was best for the company.

I blame part of this number fixation on Wall Street and the quarterly results it demands. "Are you going to hit your numbers?" becomes the defining question for any CEO, but it's the wrong question, emphasizing short-term results—which can be manipulated anyway—over the long-term performance of the company. Nonetheless, any CEO in America will have hell to pay if earnings do not meet the Street's expectations.

Companies also have themselves to blame, as they blithely misuse numbers or fail to recognize their limitations—in many cases, the numbers are contrived projections of a reality that does not exist. Spreadsheets have made this possible.

Yes, some managers live and die by spreadsheets, but I'm convinced they will be corporate America's undoing. They've already destroyed Japan and will soon destroy China, because those great countries send us their talented MBA students and take back with them our spreadsheets.

I have a long history with spreadsheets. When I was in graduate school in the early 1980s, I used the first personal-computer spreadsheet, called VisiCalc, for "visible calculator," and I used it on my DEC Rainbow. The spreadsheet allowed you to do things that you couldn't do before. You'd put numbers in their own cell, hit "recalc," and get your results. If you changed any of those numbers, you'd toggle over and hit "recalc" again, and you'd get your new results. This "visible calculator" was a powerful way to build models, but in one critical respect, it was no different from any other calculator: the results were only as good as the numbers you put in, and those numbers were only as valid as the assumptions behind them.

At the request of one of my professors, I used VisiCalc to build a model on the sharing of health care costs between union and management, which could be used in contract negotiations. The thinking was, if the two sides could accurately project changes in this key benefit, the negotiations would be smoother. I was proud of the model, and my professor took it to the UAW in Detroit . . . where it was immediately rejected. The union said benefits were nonnegotiable. Regardless, I thought this new way of calculating and displaying numbers was really cool.

It was only the beginning. Spreadsheets became a lot more sophisticated—Excel became the most popular—and now you could just change a number in a cell, and the outcomes would automatically adjust. No "recalc" button. That was significant, symbolically as well as operationally, because now you could tinker with individual numbers, easily and seamlessly, to get different results. It practically invited abuse. Instead of focusing on your inputs—and the many assumptions and sensitivity analyses behind them—you'd ask yourself: what outcome am I seeking, and then you'd adjust those inputs accordingly. As the spreadsheets became more powerful, they could accommodate entire silos of data and perform more abstruse calculations, and now you could build larger and more intricate models, all buttressed by layers of hidden assumptions and obscure formulas.

And that was the problem. A spreadsheet doesn't tell you what's going on three levels below the numbers. It doesn't tell you what assumptions were made, or the sensitivity around those assumptions, or what trend lines were excluded, or what risks were ignored. And yet we believe the numbers as if they were generated by the divine—these are the false gods of Excel.

When someone comes to me with a spreadsheet, I ask all kinds of questions, but it comes down to this: what do you really believe to be true, and what's bullshit?

I once had an executive come into my office and, with spreadsheet in hand, ask me for $40 million for a new initiative.

"Here's the deal," I said. "Are you confident that you're going to hit those numbers?"

"I know I can," he said.

"Great," I said. "You give me your home mortgage, and I'll give you the $40 million. That's the trade. If you meet these numbers, I'll personally pay off your mortgage. But if you miss the numbers, I own your house. Do you still want the $40 million?"

He thought about it briefly.

"No," he said.

Why not?" I asked.

He told me that, well, there was this risk and there was that risk, and there were all kinds of things beyond his control that could go wrong.

"Fine," I said. "Come back to me when you've got the real numbers."

I've made that mortgage offer to several members of my team. No one has ever taken me up on it.

I'm not saying that most people try to deceive or mislead—they don't. My point is that spreadsheets are so easy to manipulate, they do not necessarily represent the truth, and even when everyone is acting in good faith, they can conceal what is really going on and lead to disaster. I know this lesson well because my misplaced confidence in one of my own spreadsheets led to one of the biggest mistakes of my career.

MY PREDECESSOR AT Aetna, Ron Williams, is a superb leader. When he joined Aetna in 2001, the company reported a net loss from continuing operations of $292 million. When he hired me in 2003, Aetna was losing a million dollars a day. Ron became CEO in 2006, and when he retired as chairman in 2011, the company's annual operating earnings were $2 billion.

Ron was numbers driven in the best sense, using factual data to ground his decisions, though he had an unconventional way of consuming the information. One day I was in his office, and I walked into a side room that I thought was a bathroom. It was his data room, in which plexiglass walls were covered with financial reports. His chief of staff would tape new reports to the walls each morning, and if Ron got nervous about something, he would go in there, turn on the light, and—sometimes using a ladder—press his nose to the wall and study the numbers. Never seen anything like it, but it worked for Ron.

As CEO, he wanted Aetna to be seen as a growth stock, and for that to happen, the company needed to consistently achieve 15 percent growth in earnings per share. It was doable, at least until the global economy collapsed in 2008. Every business, ours included, was deeply affected, but we didn't scale back our operating plan for 2009. That plan, as we were putting it together, still projected 15 percent growth. I got very uncomfortable with it because, among other things, it called for massive layoffs. I finally went into Ron's office and shared my concerns.

"I've got a plan here to reach our 15 percent," I said, "but it calls for laying off 5,700 people [out of 45,000]. It's going to happen in the first quarter of next year, so it's 'Happy holidays, and here's your pink slip.' If you do that, I think it's going to damage the company in a lot of ways, and if you're really going to do that, I want to be the first to go."

A reduction of that magnitude, I thought, would destroy what we had been working to build. So, at Ron's behest, we developed two other operating plans, and Ron agreed to a new goal of increasing earnings per share by 13.25 percent.

That would require laying off about 2,800 employees, which was still a lot of people, but we could at least do it by delayering the organization and not hurting it.

Even with the projected layoffs, we had to keep running the numbers through the spreadsheet to get to 13.25 percent; we recycled those numbers three times, and we kept saying to ourselves, What assumptions do we need to believe to get to our earnings target? We kept plugging in the numbers until we got to a projected 13.25 percent; we forced ourselves to believe in our assumptions, and no one was there to stop us.

Our earnings estimate was higher than those of our peers, who were at 6 or 7 percent. The Street didn't believe us— this remained the worst economy since the 1930s—and after Ron offered his 2009 guidance, our stock got hammered. We announced our layoffs in the first quarter of 2009, and we appeared to be on track for the year. But in the second quarter, health care costs began to rise in ways that we had never seen before. Something was very wrong.

The economy had already cratered, with companies across the country slashing their workforce. When that happens, people who are about to lose their jobs seek additional medical care while they are still covered by their employer, and that intensity of service increases insurers' costs. We badly underestimated that impact. We also did not anticipate the extent of our COBRA losses. COBRA is the federal law that requires employers to continue health coverage of terminated employees, who are also motivated to use additional medical care before that coverage is gone. Our loss ratio on COBRA is 150–200 percent of premiums, and we typically have 1–1.5 percent COBRA membership. But in 2009, that number shot up to 3.5–4 percent. Then, under TARP (the Troubled Asset Relief Program), the federal government extended COBRA coverage from eighteen months to thirty-six months, increasing our costs and deepening our losses.

We saw a 12 percent increase in medical costs the second quarter of 2009. We hadn't seen anything close to that in decades. It was like the end of *Harold and Maude,* with the car going off the cliff. We were all going off the edge, which none of us anticipated. If someone had told me in the fourth quarter of 2008 that costs would rise by 12 percent, I'd have said you're crazy, and if we had to price for it, our customers would have killed us.

But as Aetna's president, I was responsible. When I went in for my midyear review with Ron, I told him, first, that we should have never agreed to a 13.25 percent earnings increase. (Our operating earnings declined by 36 percent in 2009.)

Ron said he agreed.

Then I said, "Before you ask me any more questions, I have just one question for you. Why am I still here? Why haven't you fired me?"

He told me, "If you're going to be a really great executive, you can't be that unless you fix things that are broken. So, I've got two choices. I can fire you, and I fix it. Or you try to fix it, and if you don't, then I'll fire you."

He said if I fixed it, I'd be the next CEO.

By then, we had already begun to repair the mess. We convened a group of forty senior managers from across five business groups, and I made the executive who was already in charge of each group responsible for the cleanup (though I led middle-market pricing, which was in the worst shape). Some leaders, in my position, would have reassigned these executives to different parts of the company, but I told the team, "You made this problem, now what are you going to do to fix it?"

Which is exactly what Ron told me.

The groups met several times during the week, and then we met on Sundays, in what I called a "bring-down," in which we discussed what we had discovered during the week, what we're doing, and what were the next steps. I had certain rules for these meetings: no cell phones, no laptops, and if you missed one of these meetings, you would not be allowed to return.

We drilled down into the numbers, and drilled some more, and we discovered that the problem was not only in misjudging the intensity of service and the spike in COBRA, but we also didn't realize that providers had hired consultants to increase their reimbursement for questionable claims. We didn't see these problems because they were two or three layers beneath the numbers. But we embraced the façade, we engaged in groupthink, and we were too eager to accept our assumptions as fact.

Once the errors were discovered, we could begin to solve them. Fall turned into winter, and everyone remained focused. I thought it would take a year to pull out of the crisis, but we did it in two quarters. After everyone returned from the holiday, I told my senior executives that they would now be moving to new positions. We had people who'd been in their jobs for many years, and I thought we needed fresh eyes on everything. Two of my executives said they couldn't make the change at this point in their careers. I told them they had to, or they'd have to quit. And they did just that.

Ron made good on his promise and, with the board's approval, made me CEO, but I had learned some important lessons. The first time I met with my senior team, someone asked me, "What are we going to commit to the Street?"

I said, "We're going to commit to 7 percent."

It was as if I had committed a heresy.

Someone said, "But we've always done 15."

I said, "It's time to adjust their thinking."

The Affordable Care Act had just been passed, and we didn't know how that would affect our earnings. The real question, however, wasn't 7 percent versus 15 percent, or growth stock versus nongrowth stock. The numbers were just numbers. We can fall into the trap of managing by the spreadsheet, and we don't ask ourselves, what do we believe in? What are we trying to accomplish? What's our mission? Once you ask and answer those questions, then you can make the tough decisions and place your bets.

When I became CEO, yes, we wanted to earn money, but not just for the next quarter or the next year. I thought that if we promised a more modest 7 percent, we would have more money to invest in our employees and our members and in the future of the business—investments that would pay off in the long run. I also wanted to strengthen the company to minimize the kinds of shocks that we experienced after the last financial crisis. Since I became CEO, whenever we've had to reduce the workforce, we've done it mostly through buyouts and have avoided large-scale layoffs.

From 2010 to 2017, Aetna's earnings per share increased on average 20 percent a year. If you believe you are doing the right thing, and if you have the right operating model, management processes, organization, and people, the numbers will be a true representation of the company's value. But the numbers are something that comes out of actual performance, not something that can be manipulated to get a predetermined outcome, and not something generated by an automatic "recalc."

3

YOU DON'T HAVE ALL THE RIGHT ANSWERS

I ALWAYS THOUGHT I KNEW ALL THE ANSWERS, AND IN some ways, that served me well. Leaders need to project confidence—if you don't believe you're heading in the right direction, no one else will follow.

Early in my career, I ran meetings with the swagger of infallibility. The night before a meeting, I'd bring home a binder of information, read all the materials thoroughly, and then write down what I thought the solutions were. The next day, I'd walk into the meeting and say, "I know what the right answers are, let's go!" They would look at me and say, "Okay, if that's what you want." Sometimes I was right, sometimes I was wrong, but either way, I adhered to my invincible judgment.

Over time, I decided that instead of telling others how to solve the problem, I would ask two or three questions that would hopefully lead them to the right answer.

Well, I got bored with that, too. In the early 1990s, I was working at SelectCare, which was a combination of an HMO and a PPO. One day, I went to a meeting with my boss and with representatives from another health care organization, a nonprofit that wanted to create a joint venture with us. They were discussing a tax law known as the inurement prohibition, which essentially says that nonprofit earnings cannot "inure" to the benefit of any private shareholder or individual. When I was in graduate school, I had published a research paper on this very tax law. I knew it cold, and I knew that, based on how we had structured the joint venture, it would not be in violation.

At this meeting, the discussion went on and on, stymied by the intricacies of this tax provision, and I just sat there quietly. I wanted to see if they could figure it out themselves. I finally stood up, walked out of the room, and returned with a *New York Times* crossword puzzle.

They all looked at me.

"What are you doing?' one of the lawyers asked.

"I'm doing the crossword puzzle," I said.

"Why?"

"I'm waiting for you guys to catch up. It's obvious you don't know the right answer. I do. When you want to know what my opinion is, you can ask me. Until then, can you help me with five-down?"

The meeting blew up. My boss eventually restored calm, and the deal was completed. But he later said to me, "Next time, can you just do a mental crossword puzzle?"

I was right about the inurement prohibition, but I was also being a jerk. I wish I could say that my experiences in the workplace eventually taught me humility, but it really wasn't that. It took a family crisis to make me realize that I didn't have the right answers to everything, a crisis that also forced me to reassess what I was actually doing with my career.

I HAD BEEN hired by New York Life to help turn around its group business, and that effort culminated in the sale of its NYLCare Health Plans division to Aetna in 1998. Aetna was already in the midst of integrating another big acquisition and didn't have a role for me, so I resigned. I didn't need to work anymore and was ready for the downtime, but I soon received a call from Cigna Corporation, whose new CEO, Edward Hanway, needed someone to upgrade his leadership team and oversee the company's service and technology operations. At forty-two, I was too young to retire, and I could only have lunch with my wife so many days a week before she got sick of me, so I accepted the job. In 1999, we moved to Avon, Connecticut, and bought an eleven-thousand-square-foot house with a hot tub overlooking the Farmington Valley. Life had never been so good.

One morning in November 2001, I was working out in our gym on the third floor, and my son, Eric, came in.

He was sixteen, a sophomore in high school with blond hair and blue eyes and—at five foot eight and 140 pounds—he was also a running back on the football team. Eric and I always had a good relationship, in a way that is true for many fathers and sons; a special bond. When Eric was an infant, I'd lie on the couch, place him on my chest, and play Bach's *Air on a G String*—certain that the beauty of the music would touch his young soul.

When Eric was two, I took him to the slopes, attached a long rope to his waist, and taught him how to ski. To ensure he was bending properly, I had him hold a broomstick at knee level. One time he was going too fast; I skied up behind him, and just as I pulled the rope he let fly the broomstick. It shattered my nose. There I lay in the snow, blood everywhere, and he stepped over to me and sweetly asked, "Daddy, should I call ski patrol now?"

By seven, Eric was an expert skier.

I also had seen Eric through tough times. As a boy, he had asthma and severe allergies, and I raced him to the hospital when he had his first massive reaction to peanut butter. Susan was engaged every day, and we worked together in convincing Eric's school district to keep EpiPens in the classroom. We also used a portable breathing machine in our home gym so he could receive his treatments while I worked out.

We had our conflicts, of course, and Eric went through a rebellious stage when I was on the road, but our differences were minor. When he was young, I'd drive him around in my Mustang, the radio cranked and the top down, and everything was fun and cool. We were also fairly open with each other. When he was fourteen, he came into my home office, sat down on the couch, and said, "Dad, we have to talk."

He was upset. "I don't want to be like you," he said. "I don't want to be a big-shot business guy. I don't want to live in a mansion. I want to be a normal person."

I asked him why.

"Because I'll never be able to do this."

He told me that he just wanted to be a teacher.

I told him that was fine. "You can be whoever you want to be, and you don't need to be me," I said. "As long as you are a productive steward of what I leave you and do what you want to do really well, then you will have lived a good life."

On that morning in November 2001, when I was working out in our home gym and Eric walked in, he teased me about Cigna's low stock price, and I noticed red spots under his arm.

"Did your mother change the detergent?" I asked. "It looks like you have a rash."

"It doesn't itch," he said.

I took a closer look and realized Eric had petechiae, or bleeding through the skin. I knew that could indicate any number of things, either minor or serious.

"We have to get that looked at," I told him.

He went in for tests, but even before we got the results, the signs were bad. We were in Vermont over Thanksgiving, and Eric got sick on the drive back home, his spleen so enlarged that he couldn't buckle his seat belt. On the following Monday, I was at my office on a videoconference call when my assistant came in.

"You have to leave immediately," she said.

"How important is it?"

"Your wife just called. Eric has cancer."

I've had the wind knocked out of me plenty of times, but I've never been so stunned, so incapable of breathing, as I was at that moment. Susan and I tried to remain hopeful that it was treatable and that Eric's life would not be altered irrevocably. Whether it's at work or at home, I'm a hands-on manager. In Eric's case, Susan and I drove to a Border's book store and bought *Harrison's Principles of Internal Medicine*, and that book became my medical bible over the long months to come. While we didn't know what kind of cancer Eric had, we did know that he had an enlarged spleen that was dying because it was full of dead T-cells, and the doctors at Hartford Hospital talked to us about removing it. *Harrison's* identified several possible causes for an enlarged spleen, and the last gave me a chill: gamma-delta T-cell lymphoma. According to the textbook, if a patient had that type of cancer and the spleen was removed before a bone marrow transplant, the patient would die.

We asked our doctors if this could be what Eric had. They said they had never seen it before but would test for it. I was at the office, and Eric and Susan were at home when I got the call on December 1: he had gamma-delta T-cell lymphoma.

Forty-seven people had been diagnosed with it. All died.

The enormity of the moment set in, and I plunged into grief and self-pity, enraged by those rogue cells sabotaging Eric's body, crushed by the unfairness of it all, and heartsick by the suffering that I knew he would endure. That protective shield, in which every parent tries to encase his child, had now been shattered. One moment, Eric was lithe and strong, racing toward the end zone, and the next moment, he was under siege, mauled by an enemy that he could not see or avoid, and the clock on his own mortality was ticking.

I wallowed in despair for a few days, and then I snapped out of it. I knew that I needed to be clearheaded, and I needed to be strong for Eric as well as Susan and our daughter, Lauren. I'd been successful in business because I knew how to solve problems. So my response to Eric's diagnosis became the same: How do we solve this?

We took Eric to the hospital, where he was placed in a room on the adult med/surgical unit. I of course had worked in an ER in my youth and had spent my entire career in the health insurance industry. That meant countless professional interactions with health care providers, hospital administrators, and industry representatives. Susan and I also had experience in dealing with pediatricians, nurses, and specialists for whatever medical issues our kids encountered. But none of that prepared me for what happens when your child is admitted to a hospital, and when that child is released—or even if that child is released—is unknown.

The doctor and I began telling Eric about his diagnosis and how serious it was.

"Am I going to miss school?" Eric asked.

"Yeah," I said. "At least a year."

"Maybe two," the doctor said.

I thought a lighthearted observation was in order. "Don't worry, Eric. It took me eight years to get through under-graduate school."

The doctor looked at me. "Oh, so that's why you're a health insurance executive?"

My face reddened. "Doctor, can I talk to you in the hallway?"

Outside, I turned to him. "I really appreciate what you've done for my son, but what are you doing?"

"What do you mean?"

"You're taking pot shots at me while we're telling my son that he's dying."

It was a minor incident, but it foreshadowed a casual in-sensitivity that we often heard from the hospital staff in con-versations with Eric. The doctors, nurses, and technicians weren't rude but seemed unaware of what Eric was experi-encing. Maybe that's inevitable when you deal with sick or critical patients all day long. You get numb. But for that and other reasons, I moved Eric to Children's Medical Center in Hartford and put him under the care of a different team.

I told the chief resident that whenever he spoke to Eric, one of his parents needed to be in the room. "I don't want you answering questions from him," I said. "He's sixteen. He's a minor, and we need to be in the room. This is a dreadful disease, and we need to help him manage this. We need to give him hope."

A couple of days later, I was sitting in my office when I got a phone call from Eric. He was in a panic.

"What's going on?" I asked.

"Dad, they say my penis won't work anymore."

"Whoa! What do you mean?"

"They said it won't work. What are they going to do? Cut it off?"

I got the resident on the phone and asked him what he told Eric.

"We're telling him that he's not going to be fertile anymore from the chemotherapy and the total-body radiation."

I sped over to the hospital and reached the doctor outside Eric's room, and I reiterated that Susan or I had to be present whenever he spoke to Eric. We walked in, and I told Eric that his treatment would make him infertile but we would collect his sperm if he ever wanted to have children.

The doctor looked at me and said, "It's probably not worth collecting. The cancer is terminal."

I grabbed him by the shoulder, walked him out of the room, and told him he was off the case.

Again and again, the same thing happened. The doctors didn't see Eric as an actual person. He was a disease, and even when they were in the room with him, they talked about him as if he weren't there. I was honest with Eric about his illness.

"This cancer has never been cured," I told him. "And I'm sorry. But you have my absolute commitment that there will be no stone unturned. We're going to find a cure for this. I will go anywhere and everywhere to try to find a way to save your life, and I'm going to make it my full-time job. This is a journey that we need to take together, and you need to be as strong as all of us if we're going to make this work."

I told Eric that if everything failed, I'd tell him that as well. "If we get to that point, I'm going to say, 'Game over.'"

I knew from the outset that this cancer was going to roil the entire family, so I hired a family psychologist. Bland Maloney (her real name) sat down with us and said that 80 percent of parents who have a child with cancer end up getting divorced, particularly if the child dies. The parents tend to blame each other. Maloney told us not to do that.

"Blame the system," she said. "The system is broken. Take on the system."

THE DOCTORS GAVE us two grim options. One was to remove Eric's spleen to minimize the pain and then take him home, where he would have at most five months to live. Or Eric could receive chemo and radiation, which might give him six to twelve months but would also be grueling. Any chance of a successful outcome, of survival, was barely discussed. As I came to understand, the entire case was a bizarre and ruthless aberration: the forty-seven known diagnoses of gamma-delta T-cell lymphoma were of men between seventeen and thirty-four. Eric was below the age threshold. He was on a frontier that no one had ever walked, let alone returned from.

We opted, of course, for the more aggressive treatment, which meant chemo treatments in January and February 2002, followed by radiation. Those would put the cancer in remission, but we were looking for a cure. That's how we found Dr. Eva Guinan.

A kind, curly-haired woman, Dr. Guinan was the head of the Bone Marrow Transplant Unit at Boston Children's Hospital, and she became a key ally not only in Eric's care but also in challenging the hospital bureaucracy as we pressed for more aggressive treatment. She explained, regarding Eric's disease, that the deadly T-cells reside in the bone marrow, which comes under assault from the chemo and radiation. Bone marrow transplants allow for heavier doses of those therapies, but the therapies, at best, can only put this kind of cancer in remission. It would soon come roaring back in the very same bone marrow.

Dr. Guinan had a novel idea. She wanted to give Eric a *bad* bone marrow transplant, or one that his body would reject. In medical parlance, it would create "graft versus host disease" such that the immune system, recognizing the invader, would attack the bad bone marrow and, in the process, destroy the cancer cells once and for all. That had never been done before, and the bad bone marrow could result in the immune system attacking not only the cancer cells but also healthy organs. Lacking any other options, we all agreed it was worth the risk.

In February 2002, on one of those classic cold, gray winter days in New England, we drove Eric up to Boston, where he was admitted into the Bone Marrow Transplant Unit of Children's Hospital. The place was sterile and bleak, with controlled air filters in each room and the aroma of Purell drifting through the halls. No matter how bright the sun might be shining, the floor was always gloomy and dim, the windows shaded, and it somehow felt as if we were all walking through a slow-motion movie. Thirteen other patients were on the floor, mostly children and teenagers, all with cancer. The patients didn't see one another, as their compromised immune systems could not tolerate that exposure, but I glimpsed the other kids from the hallway. All angelic, in their own ways. There was the two-year-old boy who was already receiving his second bone marrow transplant, and there was the nineteen-year-old girl who was making her fourth visit to the unit—her family knew this time she would not make it out alive.

The parents saw one another in the hallway and waiting room. We sometimes had bagels and coffee together, and we'd share notes about treatments and therapies. But we were all on separate, lonely journeys with our own children, and we didn't have the emotional bandwidth to invest in the fate of every child. But we could still pity. The doctors had told us that Eric's cancer was the worst, and some of the parents expressed their regrets to me.

We tried to keep up Eric's spirits. On his first night, he and I, along with a friend of his, began playing video war games at 7 p.m. We kept rotating the control panel, ordered in pizza and sodas, whooped it up when we shot the bad guys, rotated some more, and played full throttle late into the night.

I looked up, and there was the nurse, looking very stern.

"I just thought I'd let you know," she said, "it's four a.m."

"Oh my God. I'm so sorry."

"You can't imagine, Mr. Bertolini, how wonderful that laughter sounds on this floor."

Eric was about to undergo five days of full-body radiation to destroy his bone marrow, but what that meant didn't hit me until we walked into the radiation room. Eric lay on a table, put on his headphones, and listened to a new Dave Matthews album. The nurses placed metal plates on his lungs so he wouldn't develop tumors. I noticed that the walls were three feet thick to ensure that none of the radioactive particles leaked out, and I suddenly realized what was about to happen: they were going to descend this large metal machine over my son's body and blast it with radiation for a full hour, like bombs on Hiroshima, and after five days his blood would not be delivering enough oxygen to his tissues, his tissues would deteriorate, and he would die, unless the new bone marrow saved him. I started thinking, *I'm letting them kill my son*, and I began to freak out. The hospital staff took me out of the room, sat me down, and gave me Valium.

After his first day of radiation, Eric returned to his room and vomited. The same thing on the second day. He had a small port in his chest through which the nurses drew blood twice a day to measure his white and red blood cell counts, platelets, hematocrit, and hemoglobin. I asked for the reports and recorded the numbers on a whiteboard next to the television, each day quantifying his decline. Chemo had already taken most of his hair, but now Eric was bald, pale, and thinning out further. The fourth day was the worst. It was March 29, Good Friday. Eric returned to his room depleted, nauseous, and nearing death. But he never complained, never asked why. Saturday, we watched what became our favorite TV show in the hospital—*Mystery Science Theater 3000,* which featured a janitor and two robots sitting in the front row of a movie theater, watching B horror films (*The Blob, The Day the Earth Stood Still, Zombie Nightmare*). The series was a goofy cult classic, but always a hit in our corner of the Bone Marrow Transplant Unit, and on this Saturday enough to bring a smile to Eric's face.

My brother Peter was the perfect match for the bad bone marrow, and for him and all other bone marrow donors, there is a special place in heaven—the procedure is brutal. Doctors drilled two hundred tiny holes along Peter's iliac crest, against the pelvic bone, and sucked out his marrow, mixed it in some solution, and poured it into a bag. Easter morning arrived, and we thought Eric would be rolled away into some special room for his lifesaving transplant. But the nurse strolled in with the bag of bone marrow, hitched it onto the pole next to Eric's bed, attached the tube, and without any pomp or blessing, delivered the fluid. The transfusion was done in an hour.

The moment wasn't lost on me. On Easter, we were trying to revive Eric from his imminent death. The hours passed, followed by days, and we watched as Eric slept and stirred. The color slowly returned to his cheeks. His blood levels rose, which I duly recorded on the whiteboard. Hair began to sprout on his head, and he was not experiencing any adverse effects.

The treatment appeared to have worked. It appeared that the intervention had killed the cancer cells, but Eric's body had otherwise accepted the bad bone marrow without attacking any other organs. We had dodged an immunological bullet, and Eric was going home.

WE OFTEN THINK that we are prepared to deal with crisis. We often say, "If X happens, I know exactly what I would do next." In fact, when X does happen, responses vary widely. Some people do exactly what they planned. Others decompensate or freeze. Most of us, I believe, rely on some combination of full-throttle engagement and careful adjustment to overcome whatever sudden hardship or threat has been thrust upon us.

That crisis framework applies to the workplace, where some people will engage and adjust while others sometimes act as if they are in a life-or-death drama. "This is the worst day of my life," they will say, or "I will lose my job because of this mess." These reactions are almost always overblown and distracting and, if spoken by leaders, can be damaging for the entire company.

Perspective matters. I have now had some truly bad days, including with Eric, and I know that nothing in the normal course of business meets anyone's test for "the worst day in my life." Why? Because with rare exceptions, no one is going to die from the things we do at work.

But our businesses still face disruptions, emergencies, and the occasional crisis, and I believe our approach in dealing with them should be similar to how we deal with those in our personal life. In either scenario, we need to be present, focused, and steady, all the more so for leaders.

Leaders can't run around with their hair on fire. They need to home in on what matters, avoid fruitless searches for perfection, and direct the team on those remedies that will work. Most important, leaders need followership . . . an understanding throughout the organization of its mission, goals, and management processes as well as a commitment to make the remedies even better than how they were initially conceived.

TWO WEEKS AFTER the transplant, Susan and I brought in pizza and had a party in Eric's hospital room. His bags were packed, but right before leaving, he stepped into the bathroom. Then he came out screaming, complaining that his entire groin area was swollen and bright red. The graft-versus-host disease was suddenly spreading across his skin, and unless the disease was arrested, the skin would literally fall off.

A specialist was summoned, and she told us we had to leave the room so she could deal with Eric directly. She knew what she was doing, and she prescribed a cocktail of drugs that required additional long, tedious days in the hospital but brought the skin ailment under control.

We now careened from one crisis to the next. The graft-versus-host disease had migrated to Eric's gastrointestinal tract, and whatever he ate, he vomited. Blisters soon appeared in his mouth. He needed nutrition, which itself shouldn't have been a problem. Patients can receive nutrients intravenously, in what's called total parenteral nutrition. But TPI contains intralipids, or fats, which are soy based, and Eric was allergic to soy. We thought that the allergy may have been neutralized because he now had someone else's bone marrow, so we gave him the TPI. Bad idea. Eric went into anaphylaxis—an extreme reaction, which forced us to give him epinephrine, and that would later damage his kidneys. The TPI also impaired his pancreas, giving him diabetes temporarily and requiring that Eric receive insulin.

Susan and I had been alternating visits—an extra bed was brought into the room, and she would stay with Eric three or four days a week, I'd be there the remainder, and whoever wasn't on call was back home with Lauren, who was a freshman in high school. She was just finding her way. She was in elementary school when we moved from the Detroit area to Franklin Lakes, New Jersey, which was a culture shock. (Franklin Lakes is where *Real Housewives of New Jersey* was filmed.) Lauren was wearing oversized Red Wing T-shirts and sweatpants while the other girls were applying nail polish. We then moved to Avon when Lauren was in middle school, and that was a better fit—the town had more residents from the Midwest. Lauren found her niche playing lacrosse and field hockey. Almost six feet tall, she was a force on the field. She also wore four-inch heels to her middle school dance, so she towered over her would-be suitors, but with long dark hair and an athlete's build, she cut a striking figure.

It wasn't necessarily easy being Eric's little sister—he was popular and had a habit of making out with Lauren's friends at school dances. They had their sibling rivalries, but the night of Eric's diagnosis, Lauren reeled with guilt about not being a better sister. The whole thing was like a bad movie. Everyone in the high school soon knew of Eric's illness, and Lauren was seen, as she later said, "as the rich kid with the dying brother."

For me, when I was at work, I really wasn't at work—I couldn't focus—so I took a leave of absence from Cigna to spend my full time with Eric. We were surrounded by chaos, with nurses parading in and out checking Eric's blood pressure, temperature, and other vitals, and with an endless stream of attending doctors, residents, interns, nutritionists, orderlies, and administrators. With my medical textbook and my laptop, I tried to stay in the eye of the hurricane. But each day, I grew more dismayed with the operation of the hospital.

Eric was connected to machines that delivered his meds, and when they reached their end point, they would beep, loudly, so the nurses down the hall could hear them. This often happened at night and woke up Eric and me, startled, to the shrilling BEEP! BEEP! BEEP! I didn't understand that. If they put the patients first, they'd build a system so that the alarm would sound only at the nurses' station.

And then there were the food issues. Eric's allergies meant that the kitchen was not supposed to serve him peas, legumes, or nuts. But some of these would slip through and make their way onto his plate. If Eric ate them, they could destroy his kidneys or even kill him. Tired of having to inspect his tray each meal, I set up a meeting with the dietician and then asked if we could go into the kitchen. I wanted to see how they identified what foods were given to Eric. We walked to the food line and reached the final checkpoint, where someone inspected each tray. And there I saw Eric's plate, with a helping of legumes!

I tapped the guy on the shoulder. "Excuse me," I told him. "My son's allergic to legumes."

"These aren't legumes," he said.

I turned to the dietician. "You've got a problem here."

I recognize that hospitals save lives every day. I also know they are pressure cookers, that doctors and nurses are overworked, and that the disparate and complex needs of all the patients create nearly infinite opportunities for error. But that is of little solace if your son is being fed food that could kill him. The more time I spent in the hospital, and the more I realized that the environment invites the inevitable mishap, the more it dawned on me that unless you absolutely have to be there, your care is better delivered elsewhere.

Eric, at one point, developed an infection in his lung cavity, and the doctors didn't know if it was a virus or some bacteria. If they treated it but guessed wrong, they could kill him. I asked the surgical resident, while we were in Eric's room, if we could get the information we needed by taking a "peek" inside Eric's body: do laparoscopic surgery, which relies on small incisions and is minimally invasive.

I went into the bathroom, and when I got out, I saw that the doctor had drawn a line right down the middle of Eric's chest.

"What's that?" I asked.

"We're going to crack his chest," the doctor said.

That would leave a zipper on Eric's body for the rest of his life.

"No, you're not," I told him.

"We're going to find out what's going on in there."

"Can't you do that with a tube?"

"We'd have to do it on both sides."

"That's right."

"Sir," the doctor said, "your son is dying. What does it matter if we crack his chest?"

"Get the attending surgeon. You're not cracking his chest."

The attending surgeon eventually showed up and asked what the problem was.

"Do you see the line down his chest?" I said.

"Yeah."

"Do you know what they were going to do?"

"No. What?"

"They were going to crack his chest to see what was going on in there."

"That's crazy."

"This kid's going to live," I said. "You mark my word on it. And he's not going to walk out of here with a zipper down his chest."

Eric, to these doctors, was a name on a chart.

"Do you know how to use a laparoscope?" I asked the attending.

"Yes, I do."

"Can you go in on each side and see what it is?"

"Yeah, sure."

"I'll sign that order."

I don't recall if the infection was bacterial or viral, but once they discovered it, they could treat it.

The weeks rolled on after Eric's bone marrow transplant, and his condition worsened. He couldn't eat much, was losing weight, and was crapping out buckets of blood. As I lay in his room one night, Eric said, "I have to go to the bathroom." I rolled the porta-potty across the floor, the wheels squeaking, and put Eric on it and prayed it wouldn't come out blood. But it did. I smelled it.

A few days later, I was driving on the Massachusetts Turnpike back to Avon, listening to Dave Matthews, when my phone rang. It was the floor nurse. She said that the hospital administrators had told her that I was being "unrealistic" and "unreasonable" about Eric's care—it had been about eleven weeks since he had been admitted, and all his vital signs were deteriorating, suggesting the inevitable. The administrators wanted Susan, who'd be replacing me at the hospital, to sign the papers to put Eric in hospice care, or DNR—do not resuscitate. The floor nurse also said that the hospital chaplain and two other nurses were now meeting with Eric.

I peeled off the highway, turned around, and drove 140 miles per hour back to Boston. No one pulled me over. If an officer had, I was going to say, "My son is dying! I need an escort!" I'll never forget that drive back. They waited until I had left the building until they initiated their plan to effectively send Eric to his death.

When I returned, they were breaking up the meeting with Eric, and I said, "Anything you decided is inappropriate. I will make any decision."

They told me I should let Eric go into hospice care.

"He's fought too hard," someone said. "Let Eric go."

"Over my dead body," I told them.

Eric's condition, in my opinion, wasn't the only factor in the hospital's desire to move him off the floor. It also opened up revenue opportunities. When you're hospitalized, your insurance will reimburse so much money for any given procedure, but there are caps on how much an insurer will pay. Eric's lengthy hospitalization meant that Children's could no longer receive additional revenue for his care. I knew the system well. I used to negotiate those contracts. But for the first time, I was sitting on the other side, and I knew that moving Eric to hospice care made financial sense for the hospital. Because Medicare pays for hospice care, Eric's move to that unit would once again generate money for Children's. No one from Children's ever told me that financial considerations motivated its decisions regarding Eric, but it's naïve to believe otherwise. Hospitals need their beds filled with paying customers.

It was now June 2002, and following our decision to sustain Eric's care, Susan, Lauren, and I moved to Boston, and we lived in the Ronald McDonald House, for families who have a child or sibling receiving cancer treatment. It robbed Lauren of summer camp, but all of our energy was focused on Eric. At some point Susan became overwhelmed by the stress, and Lauren was unhappy about her long summer in the hospital. The whole family was paying a price.

Eric, of course, was suffering the most, denied the most basic pleasures. The doctors had told us that Eric could not drink milk. I don't recall the reason, just that milk could kill him. But Eric loved milk, and denying it was a big loss. Then one day, when the hospital priest was visiting, Eric saw an opening. "I'm dying," Eric told him. "I'd just like a glass of milk."

The priest found some milk and was heading back to his room. I saw him in the hall and ran toward him.

"What are you doing!" I yelled.

"He just wanted some milk."

"That could kill him!"

The priest said he didn't realize and apologized.

And then the other kids on the floor began to die. One child this week, another one that week. I would hear about it from the nurses or the other parents, and we'd hug and offer solace, and pray that our kids would find passage out of there.

One night I was in Eric's room watching the Detroit Red

Wings play in the Stanley Cup Finals. We were both huge fans. The Red Wings had won the championship twice in the last five years, and on that night when we were in the hospital, when the final buzzer sounded and the Red Wings mobbed one another in celebration, I looked over to Eric, asleep, bald-headed, wearing his Red Wings jersey. I woke him up and said, "We won again."

Eric's friends from New Jersey and Connecticut donated blood and platelets, as did Susan, Lauren, and I. But the transfusions offered only temporary relief. Eric was losing his total volume of blood each day. His weight dropped to eighty pounds. The whiteboard now documented his declining albumin level, which is a proxy for nutritional status and a marker for starvation. One night, Eric had a cardiac episode and almost died. Other nights, he hallucinated: smiley faces, painted on the ceiling, were telling him that his time had come. Other times, he imagined that his grandfather was with him in the bed. To ease his pain, Eric was put in a room with color lights across the ceiling and given marijuana pills.

The surgeons decided to do an exploratory laparotomy, in which the abdomen is opened and the organs are examined. They found sores all along the GI tract, which was bleeding out dramatically. This is what happens in starvation. The gut was eating itself. The surgeons removed some of the damaged tract as well as his appendix, then sewed him back up.

When I saw the surgeon, he told me that Eric's decline could not be reversed.

"How do you know?"

"It's too far gone. He's going to lose his gut."

The attending doctor urged us once again to move Eric into hospice care.

Eric didn't need any medical reports to know what was happening. The continuous loss of blood drained him emotionally as well as physically, and one night in July, he looked at me and started to cry. "Dad, it's not going to stop."

The following morning, on July 15, the medical staff had put a blanket over the window in the consultation room, and they invited us in to talk about hospice care.

I then went to speak to Eric.

"I'm sorry," I told him. "It was a good fight, and I'll miss you."

I paused.

"But game over."

"I'm tired," he said.

It felt like we were on the Bataan Death March, with so many of the kids on the floor dying, and now Eric's time had come.

I went downstairs to the chapel, pulled out my rosary, and started praying. I don't believe any parent would give up on a child until that child has taken his final breath. The Jesuits had taught me that you're not supposed to make deals with God, but I didn't care.

"I want his life for mine," I said. "I want his pain. I want his disease. Let him live and enjoy the life that I've had."

AFTER I RETURNED from the chapel, I met with members of Eric's medical staff, and they asked me what happened to my *Harrison's* textbook and my laptop. None of that worked, I said. They believed that Eric's cancer was killing him, but I told them that I thought he was starving. His albumin level was 0.8 g/dL, while the normal range is 3.5 to 5.5. He needed nutrition, which for him was a non-soy-based intralipid, and if we could find one—and also find a way to stop his GI tract from bleeding—he could live.

A resident who was in that meeting said she would call a former professor of hers at Johns Hopkins who was a nutrition expert. Meanwhile, Susan pointed out an article about Premarin, an estrogen medication that has been used to stop the bleeding of the ureter in kidney transplants. That was the study. Both the ureter and the kidney are smooth muscles, like the GI tract. We asked if Premarin might work for that as well. What did we have to lose?

The hospice care unit was in the same building but on a different floor, and the room had nicer furnishings and a good TV. Eric had four or five days to live and would receive fluids, as dehydration is one of the most painful ways to die. Lauren met with Eric to plan his funeral and discuss what to do with his stuff. He told Lauren where he had some pot stashed in his bedroom, so she could ditch it without Susan or me knowing.

Lauren came out of his hospital room and said, "I think he's okay, Dad." Eric, too weak to continue and shriveled to seventy pounds, had accepted his death.

Lauren called our family in Detroit, and Eric's grandparents, aunts, uncles, and twelve first cousins came to Boston and participated in a bedside mass. I brought up our golden retriever, Dakota. Everyone was stunned by what they saw. My brother John said that Eric looked like something out of Auschwitz. The priest delivered Eric's last rites. Each family member held a prayer card and whispered something in his ear before leaving, but I don't believe Eric was even aware of it. He seemed at peace.

Eric had been diagnosed eight months before and had been in Boston for four months, and during that time I had never been more homed in, more determined. I studied my textbook, I got a membership to the Longfellow gym, and I didn't touch a drop of alcohol. I gave Eric a sponge bath each morning, I read the paper or watched TV, and I went to Au Bon Pain for breakfast. It was the rhythm of life, but with higher stakes.

Eventually, however, I had turned into a hospital parent. Children's Hospital actually gave me my own photo ID to hang around my neck, but the picture, taken when I first arrived, now looked different from the face in the mirror. I had become gaunt and pallid, my hair starting to turn gray. My sister Angela later told me that I had aged twenty years.

I was also tired, and on the night of Eric's bedside mass, I slept next to him and played in my mind Bach's *Air on a G String*.

The Premarin did stop Eric's bleeding, but it didn't heal the scars on his GI tract, so he still couldn't eat. Eric was down to his last couple of days when I was standing outside his room, and the resident with the Johns Hopkins connection ran up to me and said the professor knew of a non-soy-based intralipid. "It's called Omegaven," she said, "and we need to get it."

We immediately rescinded the DNR order, and Eric was given supportive treatment.

The drug was made by a German company and manufactured in Austria, but it was not approved for the United States. Though Eric was now receiving supportive care, we were in a race to get the drug before he could no longer be revived.

The chief medical officer at Cigna called the Food and Drug Administration, which told him about a compassionate-use exception for nonapproved drugs. The next day, I flew down to Washington, made a beeline to the agency, and asked for the compassionate-use form. (It's available online now.) I flew back to Boston and gave it to Eric's doctor, who had never even heard of such a form. Before approving it, the Children's Hospital Institutional Review Board handed me a twelve-page document and told me that my lawyer should review it.

I signed it and gave it back. When your son is dying, the fine print can wait.

The company that makes Omegaven is Fresenius Kabi, and we called them up. Its CEO was about to fly to the States, so he just brought the drug with him and then sent it to Boston. A week after we learned of the drug, we now had it in our possession. But when I told Eric, he wasn't sure that he wanted it.

"Dad, I'm so tired," he said. "I thought we said 'game over.'"

"This could really work," I told him. "I'll tell you what. I'll give you an incentive. A car of your choice when you get home."

So, in October, Eric began receiving the Omegaven intravenously.

And once again, we waited. Within a day Eric's albumin level rose. That's what I was watching. It was up to 1.0. Then 2.0. And 3.0. And after about a week, 4.0. He was no longer starving to death. His color came back. He stopped crapping blood. He slowly gained weight.

With the bone marrow transplant, Eric had come back from the dead, but that was carefully planned. That had precedent. This rebirth required a magic potion from some distant land, something out of a fairy tale or more likely the Bible. What occurred was a miracle.

Winter returned to Boston, and Eric left the hospital on February 18, 2003, a year after he was admitted. I also made good on my promise. When Eric got home, I bought him a BMW 325i. But our joy was tempered: the children on Eric's floor continued to die. One blond girl with curable leukemia went home, but her parents had the roof shingles changed, which set loose fungus that infected her lungs. She returned to the hospital, but her immune system was so suppressed she could not combat the infection. She fought hard but died, and I came to realize that when it comes to cancer, *curable* is a fragile term.

The Bataan Death March had claimed them all. According to our nurse, of the thirteen patients who were on the floor when Eric was admitted, the patient least likely to survive— Eric—was the only survivor. And to this day, he remains the only person in history to survive gamma-delta T-cell lymphoma. I get calls, sometimes in the middle of the night, from parents whose children have been diagnosed with cancer, seeking help. I share all that I know, but it's never enough.

THE ORDEAL SHOOK ME on many levels. For starters, it revealed shortcomings in how our health care system treats patients and in how we even define health—which was jarring for someone who had spent his entire career in the field. Doctors repeatedly treated Eric as a collection of symptoms, not as a whole person. His emotional well-being, his mental health, his aspirations—none of these were really of interest to them. The thinking seemed to be, if we can eradicate Eric's cancer, he'll be ready to return to the world, because that's what our health care system is designed to do.

But that's not nearly enough. Eric's experience began my

rethinking of what it actually means to be healthy in America, and I vowed to do something about it.

Eric's ordeal also proved that you should never succumb to the "givens" when you have a clear mission in mind.

Given Eric's particular disease and given what the doctors had told us, Eric should not have survived. He had no chance. But I wouldn't accept that. I would not let the numbers obscure the mission, and the mission was saving my son. That trumped all other considerations. I wondered how many children have died because the system had convinced their parents that their kids were doomed. It's a chilling thought, but also a reminder that advocacy—and I mean relentless advocacy—is a family's number one responsibility in our health care system.

Eric's experience humbled me as well. I always had the belief that I had the ability, as well as the resources, to control my own destiny and that of my family. But those resources did not prevent Eric from getting cancer, nor did they really save him. They helped, of course. But beyond his own strength and courage, what saved Eric was a group of people taking extraordinary measures, giving their time, energy, wisdom, prayers, and blood, to keep Eric alive and then to find a miracle cure. That shattered my belief, belatedly, that I knew all the right answers, and I just had to wait for other people to catch up. Not this time. I had to be more of a learner. I had to listen more. I had to be more open-minded. I had to accept that it wasn't about me but it was about the experts around me who could help Eric. I was Eric's chief advocate, yes, but even an advocate has to know when to be a wingman, and I took that lesson with me when I returned to work.

Over the years, Eric has continued to battle through ailments and setbacks. The immunosuppressants had badly damaged his kidneys; so in 2007, I donated my left kidney to him.

But Eric's cancer has not returned, and he's continued to thrive in his personal and professional lives. He had worked for a large bank in Boston, running the benchmark analytics department, but he returned to school in New Hampshire and is now seeking a doctorate in neuroscience and mathematics. He's going to be a teacher.

In 2016, Eric announced his engagement to his girlfriend, Lee, but they had to move up their wedding date when they discovered she was pregnant.

Eric was supposed to be infertile. What do doctors know?

At the wedding, the priest who comforted Eric in the hospital officiated the ceremony, and the band played Bach's *Air on the G String*.

4

COMMUNICATING IN THE AGE OF SOCIAL NETWORKS

WHEN I WAS AT CIGNA IN 2000, BEFORE ERIC GOT SICK, I was given an early BlackBerry—a beta version. Few people knew that I had it, and even fewer knew what it was. One day I was in the executive conference room with thirty-five other executives, and everyone was going around the table reporting their numbers. I was using my BlackBerry to type questions to my staff, who then emailed the answers. I was sitting across from my boss, who was maniacal in his focus. At one point he stood up and said, "Hold on a minute. I have to make a phone call."

He left the room briefly and then returned, but he then asked if we could wait a minute before we resumed. I noticed that he was looking straight at me. Then I looked at my email, and in came a message from his secretary: "Put the fucking toy away."

I looked up at him.

He smiled and said, "Now."

I thought I was being productive, but I wasn't about to cross swords with this guy. I put down the BlackBerry.

After the meeting, I went to his office, showed him the device, and explained how it worked. He was blown away. "This is amazing!" he said. "You can actually do all that on this thing?"

Showing him my new phone was one of the worst things

I ever did. The following week, he got his own BlackBerry, and he immediately started sending me an endless stream of emails—he could be in a meeting, in a car, on a plane—it didn't matter. He just kept sending, more and more, a Niagara of urgent demands and requests, until I realized he had become addicted to the very thing he had initially despised.

I learned early on that with communication technology, more is not necessarily better—and it may not even be more, if the communication is more about distraction. (That's why, during our Sunday Aetna meetings in 2009, I banned cell phones and laptops.) The challenge for leaders of any organization, and it was certainly my challenge, is to understand how the Digital Age is changing our work environment and then how we can use it to our advantage.

The term itself, the Digital Age, is too vague to be meaningful. What we've really created, through the Internet and handheld computers, are social networks that instantaneously connect us to people, places, and ideas that were previously beyond our reach (or to a colleague's secretary sitting on another floor). On one level, it is an amazing gift, and we should celebrate the opportunities that this has created. A while back, I needed to buy two travel bags, so I went online and found a guy in Los Angeles who's an immigrant from the Philippines. He works in an abandoned house that he converted to a factory, and based on my needs, he used Italian leather to customize my travel bags, with my name inscribed. He emailed me pictures before he sent them, and he included a personal note in the package. The Internet made a complex purchase easy and comparatively cheap, while the experience also made a mockery of the glossy brand-name retailers who've been trying to convince me that I'm getting a bargain on their leather travel bags.

That fluidity of information, that ability to connect across cities, time zones, and even continents, has radically changed how all companies must operate. We no longer have command-and-control hierarchies in which leaders could husband information, release tidbits as they saw fit, and then expect employees to accept those morsels as truth. To be sure, it was never quite that easy—leaders have always had to build credibility with their organizations so their messages were embraced. What's different now is how easily leaders can be exposed. Employees know what's happening with their competitors, they know what's happening in other markets, and they know what's happening with me, with you, and with any other supervisor or manager. Websites allow employees to rate their bosses, compare salary levels, and evaluate corporate cultures. It's all out there, one click away. If you describe a new workplace benefit as "unique," a new product as "groundbreaking," or a new executive hire as "renowned," your employees will quickly discover whether that's the case, and if it's not, your credibility will be shot.

The ground rules have changed. Employees can quickly find their own version of the truth. It may just be another point of view, an opinion, a meme, an image, an idea: all of which we as executives must compete with in getting our own messages out.

Employees also have a greater opportunity to hold their managers accountable when they've been harassed or violated, and we've seen that accountability in the #MeToo movement. In the past, women really didn't have a way to speak out on their own and know that their words would be heard beyond the four walls. But social media messages that go viral have changed all that, and for the better.

Communication is one of those corporate buzzwords that

have been around for ages, more often preached than practiced. But I don't think it's an option anymore for a successful leader. Our companies are now social ecosystems, so any leader who fails to be conspicuously transparent is surrendering to the outside (digital) masses. What's more, being communicative is not just the ability to express oneself but also to listen, in an attempt to ultimately gain empathy or understanding. In my own journey, I was never at a loss for words, but over time, I learned how to use those words more thoughtfully and to hear them from others more respectfully.

SHORTLY AFTER I became CEO of Aetna, I received a call from George David, who had retired two years earlier as the CEO of United Technologies Corporation in Farmington, Connecticut. George had a phenomenal run at UTC: in 1993, the year before he became CEO, the company earned $437 million; by 2007, his last full year at the helm, UTC earned $4.2 billion, an increase of 860 percent. Jim Cramer on CNBC once called George "the best industrial CEO of the decade." But most people have never heard of him. His company ran circles around another industrial behemoth in Connecticut, General Electric, but while some of GE's top leaders became household names, George remained out of the spotlight.

George was kind enough to spend a day with me and offer guidance on being a CEO. Perhaps the biggest takeaway was what I should *not* be doing: I should not be flying off every other week to a CEO conference, confab, or country club gathering, where CEOs sit around and talk about all the difficulties of being a CEO. Stay out of that circuit, George said. It's seductive, but it diverts your attention from your business, which you will need to master. And indeed, George knew everything about his company. Aetna had a corporate helicopter, a Sikorsky S-76, which was built by UTC, and George told me about its twin turboshaft engines, its main and tail rotors, and its retractable landing gear.

I got the message. To truly understand the business, I'd have to immerse myself in the details, stay focused, and understand how everything works. I couldn't do that through briefing papers alone. I'd have to get out of the office, meet regularly with employees, and ask them about their issues. In a world that was being connected through social networks, I'd have to find new and innovative ways to connect with our employees, because if I didn't, someone else would.

That created different challenges for me than for Ron Williams, who ran Aetna when the Internet was just in the early stages. Ron gave me brilliant advice on many things, including management processes and guarding against complacency. "The leading cause of failure," he told me, "is success." But we were also very different in how we interacted with others. I liked to meet colleagues and associates for dinner, where we told stories, talked about our ideas, and laid the groundwork for what we could do during business hours. That wasn't Ron's style. He was always proper and measured in how he communicated with his subordinates. He considered keeping one's distance a virtue, as that distance, emotional as well as physical, added mystique to the corner office. Personal and professional boundaries were sacred. Between the time I joined Aetna in 2004 and was named its CEO in 2010, I'd had dinner with Ron three times.

That formality was evident in how Ron conducted his board meetings. When members of his executive team participated in those meetings, we were not allowed to speak unless we were authorized, and we were not allowed to email the directors (none of whom worked at Aetna). Ron also kept two board meeting books. In one, the corporate secretary had put tick marks next to the names of directors who were seen talking to one another during the meeting. Enough tick marks could signal possible opposition against the chairman, even a fledgling cabal. The other book was a seating chart, which was used to separate the board members who had spent too much time talking to one another.

Ron gave me both books when I became chairman in 2011.

Ron's style worked for Ron, but it wouldn't work for me. Part of the reason, of course, was that I have a different personality. To put myself in a position to get the top job, I started wearing a coat and tie to work every day, and I shaved, and I played that role. But once I became CEO, I reverted to jeans and stubble. That informality shaped my relations with the board. I didn't care which director was talking to which director—my feeling was, if you have something to say, let's hear it. Put it on the table. Let's get the conversation going. I also didn't care where the board members sat. I told them, "You're adults. You figure it out." (They decided to sit on one side of the table so they could see the management team on the other side.) Emails were now allowed. My executive team communicates with directors all the time, and they go out with them for lunches and dinners as well.

Beyond having a personality different from Ron's, I also didn't believe that you can create boundaries between directors and executives, or among the directors themselves. (I got rid of the two books.) I also don't believe that you can create boundaries between your employees and the outside world.

Those boundaries don't exist anymore, crushed by social networks; the best response is to fill those networks with your own ideas, aspirations, and values.

Or blogs.

In 2007, after I became president at Aetna, I wanted to write an internal blog so I could talk to employees directly. Ron initially opposed the idea, as did other senior executives. They thought employees would be on it too long or that it would be a distraction and reduce productivity. I said, "Go to their desks. They've got a computer and a phone, and they're using both. We can't prevent that. The four walls don't exist anymore, so let's roll with it."

I started blogging, posting on our intranet almost every month, on a wide range of topics: on the role of well-being in daily life; on business results; on the need to embrace diversity; on thanking employees for special achievements. But these were not one-way conversations or mandates from on high, which would just be another internal memo, easily ignored. I used the blog to throw out questions and start conversations, and employees responded by the droves.

I'd write, they'd respond.

Write, respond.

Write, respond.

Anonymity was not allowed. If you wrote something, your name automatically appeared. That kept out the offensive comments, but employees were still candid about what we as a company needed to be doing better, and even when we disagreed, our exchanges were respectful.

The blog was a huge success in opening up channels of communication that had never before existed, and it wasn't just a channel between employees and me but among employees who worked in different parts of the country and indeed the world. Senior executives were reading it as well. Even Ron acknowledged how important the blog had become, noting, "There's a lot of good information on there."

When I became CEO, I wanted to be much more visible in the company, and I wanted to have cultural impact. I told my PR team, "You cannot protect me. You must prepare me. So, get ready. I'm going out there and speaking truthfully and will talk about how to move forward."

I began doing town meetings at work sites around the country. When executives had done these meetings in years past, sometimes they would plant questions to ensure that they addressed certain topics—or, more likely, to ensure that at least some questions were asked, in case everyone else was too fearful.

When I did my first town hall, my staff asked me if I wanted questions planted. I said hell no. "If people don't want to ask me questions, I'll sit there and stare at them." Sure enough, at the first meeting, I opened it up for questions, and no one raised their hand. I mean, nothing. So, I said, "We've got twenty minutes together. Do you want me to do hand puppets? You ain't going nowhere until you ask some questions."

A woman raised her hand, she asked the first question, I answered, and no one got fired. More questions followed, and more followed that, and we did it again at other meetings, and employees soon realized it was safe to ask me tough, challenging questions. I would do about four town halls for each earnings report per quarter, and I would do four to six town hall meetings throughout the year at site visits. There, I'd walk through the offices and talk with frontline employees. I believe these efforts helped our employees understand what we as a company were trying to do and where we were trying to go. More important, they helped me understand what was actually happening in our business units, in our offices, in the field, and on the front lines. It's where I could gather information to marshal the ideas and energy of all our colleagues. I think it also built trust between me and the rest of the organization. Every big company will have some disillusioned employees at any given moment, but those are the exception. Most employees, I believe, want to make their companies better and will feel far more invested in the mission if their voice is heard.

I've continued writing the blog, which migrated to an internal social media platform called Jive, and it's had unintended benefits. In 2017, for example, our proposed acquisition of Humana had just been blocked by the Department of Justice. We had invested eighteen months in what would have been a transformative deal for us, and spirits were understandably low. At an off-site meeting with my senior team, I reminded everyone that we were still making good progress across all our businesses and that our employees had rallied through this time of uncertainty. My chief of staff, Steven Kelmar, asked how we could reward our employees for their efforts. Well, that year the Fourth of July fell on a Tuesday, so I asked how much it would cost to give our 49,500 employees Monday off as well. We'd have to have our nurses where we needed them, and we'd have to pay them and others overtime to maintain essential operations. But those costs, I thought, were worth it, so I made the announcement on my blog that July 3 would be a company day off. The response was amazing! During and following the long holiday weekend, Jive was bristling with employee photographs of their families at picnics and weekend retreats, celebrating the extra downtime.

It was a reminder that the blog had evolved from a strict communications initiative to being part of a digital town square of discussion and inquiry to, finally, a gathering spot of shared memories.

The personal thanks rolled in, and I knew that whatever that extra day cost Aetna in dollars and cents, it more than paid off in the goodwill and loyalty it generated among our workers.

COMMUNICATING DIRECTLY to employees was one step. I also wanted to communicate to our members, and I was going to do that through Twitter.

Over the years, I had tried to respond to letters or emails that conveyed legitimate concerns or complaints. If I didn't respond to them with my own letter or email, I at least made sure to address the problem with my team. Twitter, of course, was far more immediate and direct, but also risky. Twitter is hardly known as a deliberative medium. It's often hostile and ad hominem; the falsehoods are rarely corrected; and if you happen to run a large insurance company, you will come in for many personal attacks.

Lauren offered sage guidance about Twitter.

"Don't do it, Dad."

I said I thought I had to.

"Okay," she said, "but remember, Twitter is not about arguing. It's about listening."

So, yes, I tweet, but what I really try to do is listen, and that can be extremely valuable. Sometimes I'll learn about company mishaps on Twitter before anyone on my own team tells me, or sometimes I'll see patterns of complaints about Aetna or about health care in general. Then there was Arijit Guha, who offered an early lesson in what this communication technology was all about.

Arijit, a married doctoral student at Arizona State University, was diagnosed in 2011 with stage 4 colon cancer, which has a survival rate of under 10 percent. Arijit had purchased an Aetna health insurance policy through his university. I was still in my early months of using Twitter, and Arijit started tweeting at me that Aetna had not covered the full costs of his treatments, including chemotherapy and surgery. I tweeted back, asking Arijit if he understood what his policy covered. That ignited a firestorm. One person tweeted, "You, sir, have blood on your hands. Man up & pay for [his] treatments, & for others like him. You don't need the $, they do."

I tweeted Arijit, "follow me," which would allow me to communicate with him through direct messaging. Once we could communicate privately, I explained to Arijit that he had bought a $300,000 policy, and that policy did not protect him against catastrophic illness or injury. I told him, "I'm looking into this. I'm going to fix this for you, but I need some time."

I asked my team to show me who has these policies with $300,000 caps. Where are they sold, and how many people have exceeded the caps. It turned out that Arizona State University was the only school that had offered these policies to its students. In addition to Arijit, the school had four students who had exceeded their $300,000 cap.

So, we called ASU and told its benefits managers about these five students. We said, why don't you pay us the premiums for an uncapped policy for these students, and we will cover all of their medical costs. ASU accepted, and we got everyone covered, including Arijit.

I sent a message to Arijit and told him how we had solved the problem for him and for four of his fellow students. Arijit then tweeted, "Thank you, Twitter world. You finally forced a CEO to do it, and he did it."

But we didn't capitulate to Twitter world. We did what was in the best interest of our members who had bought policies that didn't work for them, and I would have done the same thing for Arijit had he sent me a letter in the mail. In fact, I've responded to many such letters and emails from members who were in similar circumstances.

I sent Arijit a message back and said, "That was incredibly unfair. That's not what we did, and you know that's not what we did."

He then tweeted an apology.

Arijit's story has a sad ending; he passed away in 2013 at age thirty-two. The headline in the *Washington Post* identified him as the "student who battled Aetna over cancer coverage."

The experience shaped how I would use Twitter. First, it's not a forum for dialogue or conversation. It is, as Lauren said, for listening. But it can also be a portal for direct communication with customers or clients. We created a Twitter team at Aetna—about twenty people, and we call them Mark's Minions. When people tweet me with complaints or problems, typically about coverage, we ask them to direct-message me. My team then works these issues, behind the scenes, all day long. I get a download from my "minions" once a week, get updates, and I know which problems have been solved and which are still in progress. Not every problem is resolved, but it's still a great way of using social media to provide more communication, more transparency, and more engagement with our members.

Whether dealing with employees or customers, that's the model, and there's really no other choice. The BlackBerry was buried by smartphones. The four walls aren't coming back. Leaders can't hide. And companies will either connect or disappear.

5

THE ROAD TAKEN

BUSINESSES TYPICALLY DEFINE SUCCESS AS A LINEAR path: create a plan, execute it, and follow the road. You can model outcomes, minimize variables, and isolate risks, and if you do all that, you can have a pretty good idea of what success looks like.

Until it looks like something very different.

Most leaders figure this out eventually. The world is too complicated, too random, too unforgiving to allow a straightline path to any significant achievement. A better metaphor is the captain at sea, vectoring through the storm, using all his skills to navigate a windswept route, only to discover that the port is very different from what he expected. Even that framework only considers external forces—the sea, the wind, the harbor. But what if the most daunting force you'll ever confront is the fragile realities of body and soul? What if your physical and emotional vulnerabilities are suddenly exposed and your entire equilibrium is sent off-kilter?

And what if the road you take is nothing like the one you imagined?

That was my road.

ERIC'S ILLNESS HAD already begun to change me. I had returned to my job at Cigna in November 2002, even before

Eric had returned home. I was running the company's field organization, and I was in a meeting for our 2003 operating plan. The company was built around the numbers, driven by the stock price and earnings, but the numbers in front of me looked one-dimensional and misleading. Thirty of us were sitting around a table, and Ed Hanway, the CEO, asked me what I thought.

I told him what I thought.

"It says we're going to grow by 2 percent, but I think we're going to be down by 8 or 9 percent."

Hanway stood up and started screaming at me, saying I had been gone all these months and was in no position to question the management team's numbers.

I put my hands on the table and asked, "Are you done screaming at me?"

"What do you mean?"

"I don't need this," I said. "If you want to have an adult conversation about what's going on, I'll be in my office."

I walked out of the room.

About twenty minutes later, Hanway walked into my office and apologized, but it was too late.

"Ed, I don't want to be here, so by the time the holidays roll around, I'll be gone. I'm done with this place." All the metrics were evidence of success or failure, but I suddenly didn't feel invested in any of them. They were just metrics. Charts. Graphs. I needed a mission. I didn't know what it was, but I knew I wasn't going to find it at Cigna.

It was about a week before Thanksgiving. By January, I was gone.

A few weeks after I had my last conversation with Hanway, I received a call from Jack Rowe, the chairman and CEO of Aetna (and Ron Williams's predecessor). He said he heard that Eric had returned home and wanted to know if I'd be interested in joining his company. I had briefly worked at Aetna after it acquired NYLCare Health Plans, and I didn't particularly like it, but both Jack and Ron assured me that Aetna had changed. In that first conversation, I told Jack that I only wanted to work for an organization that was mission oriented. He told me to come in and talk to everyone, and I could decide for myself. I did, and I accepted the job.

BY 2003, ERIC had been out of Children's Hospital for a year, but he was still immune deficient. While he was receiving IVIG (intravenous immunoglobulin) in Hartford, he had the first of his two strokes. In the process of recovering from the first, his brain reorganized itself, and it made him much smarter in math. A setback with a positive outcome. Eric's second stroke, in early 2004, temporarily left him unable to remember words; Lauren visited him in the hospital and used flash cards to rebuild his vocabulary ("giraffe" . . . "dog" . . . "cat"). In between the strokes, Eric slipped, cut both knees, and had to be taken to the hospital to stop the bleeding, the steroids having made his skin porous and vulnerable.

It felt as if we were trapped in a cyclone of hardship. Susan's father, Jim, had died in 2000, and three years later, my dad developed an upper respiratory infection that briefly put him in a medically induced coma. In February 2004, I left for Detroit to visit him in a nursing home where he was receiving rehabilitation, and there, I saw him cry for the first time. I flew to a business conference in Scottsdale, Arizona, held at one of my favorite hotels, the Desert Princess. I finally had a moment to relax, and I thought, *This is nice, but this really isn't where I want to be.* We hadn't been skiing all season because of Eric's illness, but now we had a trip planned, and surely a few days in the mountains would be the perfect tonic for our family. Before I got on the plane to return home, I called my dad.

"Don't worry," I said to him. "Everything is going to be okay."

I flew to Hartford and picked up the family, and we drove to Killington, Vermont, where we had been going for years. We were building a new place on the mountain and were now renting a condo, where Eric, still not strong enough to ski, mostly stayed. Susan joined us on the slopes at times, but on this day, it was Lauren and I on the trails, Lauren riding her snowboard. She was still mastering it—she considered herself a traitor for shunning skis—and when she'd get stuck, I'd throw her my pole.

Lauren and I did our "ten by ten"—ten mountain runs before 10 a.m.—before the stragglers, many of whom were still hungover, clogged the trails. We then met Susan for a late breakfast at the lodge. It just felt good to do the things that we loved to do, and I was giddy, playing "Mr. Mittens" with Lauren over breakfast, putting my mittens on and having them talk to her.

Our ski day was typically over at this point, and our plan was to get out the snowshoes and go hiking with the dog. But Lauren and I decided to do one more run. It was our only ski trip of the year, and we wanted to make the most of it. Susan wasn't happy about it.

"You're nuts," she said. "You're not a kid anymore. Be careful up there."

We skied down to the lift and ascended to the top of Bear Mountain, and the conditions were perfect—high sun, little wind, good snow.

It was February 18, 2004, exactly one year after Eric had been released from the hospital.

I was a black-diamond skier who craved the rush of adrenaline, and barreling down gullies or leaping across ridges, I'm confident on the slopes. Now on this warm day, I hugged the tree line in search of powder. Bent at the waist, with my hands behind my back and my poles straight up, I shot down the mountain, and as I leaned into a turn, I heard Lauren call out from behind. I looked over my shoulder and saw her eyes widen.

That's the last thing I remember.

My ski caught an edge, and I flung headlong into the woods, smashing into a tree and hitting it flush at the junction of my neck and shoulder. My scapula split down the middle. Tumbling headfirst thirty feet down a ravine, I landed in a frigid creek, my neck broken, my left lung damaged, my head concussed, my skis hanging from frozen branches. I was wearing my helmet, but that couldn't protect the rest of my body, and even a helmet doesn't fully protect the head.

Lauren didn't know what happened. I was there, then I wasn't there. She boarded over to where she last saw me and stepped down the hill, where I was splayed in the creek. She thought I was playing a joke—she even laughed, as it's the kind of prank I would have pulled—and she waited for me to stand up.

But I didn't move. Fearing I was dead, Lauren screamed for help. Other skiers responded and made their way down the hill. No sixteen-year-old should have to live through such an experience, but Lauren was better prepared than most. She had received leadership training at summer camp and had been taught that when a person has fallen and is not moving, that person's head should not be moved. When someone was getting ready to lift me from the water, Lauren yelled, "Don't move him! Don't move him!"

Someone called the ski patrol, and as they were waiting, I remained unconscious but started mumbling, "Where am I? What happened? My left arm really hurts."

At least I was alive.

The ski patrol reached us, strapped me to a plastic sled, and tried to pull me out. But given my condition and the slick terrain, it took two hours, and I tipped over at least once. I made it up the hill and then down the mountain—they blocked off the entire trail—and all the while I was still babbling. Lauren called Susan and told her I'd been in an accident, and she met my strapped-in body at the base of the mountain. An ambulance drove us seventeen miles to a hospital in Rutland, but I was too damaged for anyone there to help me, so they medevacked me thirty miles across the New Hampshire border to the Dartmouth Hitchcock Medical Center.

There I lay for six days. At Susan's behest, I had my last rites read to me. When I did come to, the first thing I heard, on MTV, was Five for Fighting's musical elegy to a century of life.

When you only got a hundred years to live.

I realized that a nurse was giving me a sponge bath.

"What are you doing?" I asked her.

"Do you know where you are?" she said.

"I'm obviously in the hospital. How do I get out of here?"

I had a massive concussion, specifically, acute subdural hematoma, with both sides of my brain filled with blood. I could not move my left arm and felt nothing from the neck down. I cracked my scapula, avulsed my nerve roots, broke vertebrae C2, C3, C5, C6, and T1, and macerated my brachial plexus, or the network of nerves that begin in the neck and branch off to form other nerves that control the upper limbs. I smashed it like a head of garlic.

I took comfort in one thought. When Eric was in the hospital, I cut the deal with God that He could take my life to save Eric's, and if this result was part of that deal, I'd take it again.

The medics who took me on the helicopter stopped by and told me that when they were trying to keep my airway open, they felt ice and snow packed down my back. They said it froze my spinal cord, which otherwise would have ruptured and left me quadriplegic or dead.

I knew, from Eric's experience, about the risks of being in the hospital. The doctor said I had to walk before I could leave. Okay, I said. I'm going to lock and load, and I'm going to start walking again, and five days later, I was out.

I still couldn't move my left arm, but the doctors thought it would recover on its own. I just needed the right physical therapy to get everything working again.

I'VE ALWAYS BEEN a workout fanatic, and starting at age twenty-two, I began recording my exercise routines in notebooks. Every wind sprint, every push-up, every bench press, I wrote down. After college, the physical activity was an antidote to a desk-bound career, but it was about more than staying healthy. I was an endorphin junkie. It was all about skiing fast, running hard, hiking to the summit—the exhilaration of pushing myself to the absolute limit, feeling that surge of adrenaline, and then relaxing. I began doing "power of ten" workouts, in which you lift weights to the count of ten, as slowly as possible, in an effort to build muscle mass. I developed seasonal programs, in which I would spend the fall building mass, the winter increasing my power, the spring paring my weight, and then by summer looking like Adonis. Nutritional supplements sharpened my physique. I was six-foot-one, 185 pounds, with 8 percent body fat, and as the years passed, my regimen remained consistent and relentless. My last recorded workout was February 17, 2004. I was forty-seven years old.

My conditioning helped me survive my ski injuries and was a factor in my bones resetting in place. I was confident I could handle any rehab, and in that first month, I worked with a physical therapist while wearing a neck brace and taking mild pain meds. I was certain that I would regain my strength and stamina, and five weeks after my injuries, I went back to work. I felt that I had to get back into the action and that it would help my physical recovery. Aetna gave me a chair with a neck brace and a computer with a one-handed keyboard.

But I was in no shape to return. Still suffering from the effects of my concussion, I sat in meetings but couldn't really hear what people were saying. It was just noise, like that *mwa-mwa-mwa* sound that adults make in the Charlie Brown television specials. In many ways, I was barely functional. I needed someone's help to put on my watch or my bracelet or to button my shirt. My dress shirts had to be sliced down the side and along the sleeve so I could put them on, and once on my body, I used Velcro to reattach the shirt.

On a snowy day in late April, I was scheduled to speak at an investor conference at the Pierre hotel in New York. I walked up onstage with a neck brace and a cane, and I got through it but did not inspire great confidence among our shareholders. My body was stiff. My neck was crooked. My speech wasn't sharp. Meanwhile, back home, I had a hard time sleeping, until one night, I bolted upright in bed. It felt as if someone had set my left arm on fire—it was neuropathic burning pain from my left ear down to my fingertips.

I screamed my ass off.

I went to neurologists and neurosurgeons. I had CT scans, injections, and nerve exams that shot my arm full of electricity. The doctors concluded that my C7 nerve route had been avulsed from the spinal cord, and the arm, which was becoming more and more atrophied, would never function again.

"What about the pain?" I asked.

The answer was painkillers, lots of them. They put me on Neurontin (3,000 milligrams a day) and on Keppra (1,500 milligrams a day). They gave me Vicodin (every four hours) and OxyContin (every eight hours). They put fentanyl patches on each buttock and, for good measure, gave me Dilaudid for "breakthrough pain." (Translation: when all the other stuff doesn't work, they give you Dilaudid.) In time I'd have so much OxyContin in my home safe, it was almost criminal. It's not hard to understand why we have an opioid epidemic. Opioids are prescribed like candy. I still experienced the pain but just didn't care anymore—I was stoned. The ineffectiveness of the meds was probably a good thing. Had they worked, I might be addicted to this day.

We kept trying. In June 2004, I had surgery to reattach or reroute the nerves in my brachial plexus, which restored some movement in my arm but did nothing for the pain.

The whole family was on the brink. Susan was frustrated by my debilitation. Eric was still recovering from his second stroke as well as the treatments for his cancer, and poor Lauren—unknown to me—was told by her grandmother that my accident was her fault. Lauren actually had a good relationship with my mom, but because Lauren was present at my fall, her grandmother made her feel responsible. Lauren had already been through hell with Eric's cancer, and now she too went into a spiral. She started cutting herself and was put on suicide watch.

The things that once brought joy to our family were now gone. Christmas was always big for us—we'd decorate the house with garlands, wreaths, lights, stockings, and a huge tree, and we'd celebrate with a home-cooked meal. After my accident, we kept the decorations in storage, didn't buy a tree, didn't go to church, and ordered takeout.

My own tailspin continued. I'd always enjoyed wine or alcohol with dinner, but now I started to drink recklessly. I loved bone-dry Grey Goose martinis, accompanied by olives stuffed with blue cheese. I grimly made my drinks each night. I wanted to numb my pain into submission, but the drugs and the alcohol were making me more depressed while triggering bad reactions and sabotaging my sleep. Susan couldn't sleep with all my restlessness, so I ended up on the couch. One night I woke up screaming, "My arm won't work! What's wrong with my arm?"

Lauren came running and tried to explain it to me. "Dad, you had an accident five months ago."

In time I would understand what was happening. We have a sympathetic and a parasympathetic nervous system, both originating in the spinal cord. The former responds to threats—the fight-or-flight response—while the latter is the counterbalance, restoring the body to rest. They work in tandem, like dance partners who keep each other upright.

But my damaged nerves severed communication between the two systems, bringing neurological chaos. When the sympathetic system was activated, my body couldn't return to its normal state—it experienced sustained increases in heart rate, arterial blood pressure, and blood glucose—and sharp pain resulted. The whole broken apparatus was like an attitude regulator. Whenever I got angry or frustrated, my left arm hurt like a son of a bitch.

I continued taking the useless pain meds, and I was drinking too much and now eating too much. I couldn't exercise, so the chiseled fitness maniac I had been my entire life was now a pasty blob. There was no remedy, no escape. That's when I started thinking about killing myself.

I'd go out at two thirty in the morning and, in my drugged-out state, get into my dark green BMW 740IL. I did love that car, and I'd peel out of the driveway and see how fast I could circumnavigate Avon. I'd jump on Highway 44, push the pedal to the metal, and—at 120 mph and with the Connecticut night flying past me—once again feel that rush of adrenaline. I was, in that moment, free. One late night, speeding on the highway through Hartford, I pulled over as I approached an underpass. With the engine idling, I stared at a guardrail protecting five cement pillars, and I sat for a full hour, saying to myself, "I need to do this. I need to do this. I'm better off dead."

A cop finally pulled up and walked to my car.

"What are you doing?" he asked.

"I'm just sitting here," I said.

"Why?"

"I'm sad."

He told me to get out of the car and asked if I was using any drugs.

I was wearing my neck brace. "I'm using pain medication," I said.

"You shouldn't be driving."

He called another officer, and they drove both me and my

BMW home. They put the car in the garage and told me to go to bed.

Susan sold the BMW the following week.

IT WOULD TAKE several more years before I could begin to manage the pain—and manage it is still all I can do—but I did experience one breakthrough in the summer after the accident, and that breakthrough changed the course of my life.

A few months after my incident with the police, a friend mentioned that to ease my discomfort, I should try cranial-sacral therapy. I'd never heard of it but was told that a therapist would lightly rub my head and spinal cord, all the way down to my butt, to get my cerebrospinal fluid flowing again, and that would somehow make me feel better. I thought it was nonsense. But Susan had heard the same thing about this therapy, and while I was making my midnight NASCAR runs around Connecticut, she asked her yoga instructor if she knew anyone who offered it. The instructor said yes, so Susan made an appointment.

It sounded too esoteric, but with nothing to lose, I agreed to go. Susan took me to a nondescript medical office—it was rented from a psychologist—and there I met my cranialsacral therapist.

Mari Arnaud didn't say all that much during that first visit, and I wouldn't learn until much later that even she doubted she could help me. I was too far gone. With my arm in a sling, my neck crooked, and my eyes glazed over, she saw me as broken. I lay down on the table, fully clothed, in a hundred shattered pieces. Mari placed her hands on my head, said a prayer, and began.

I now understand that no health care provider, trained by

Western standards, could have helped me. My pain did not fit into any conventional box. Mari drew from a very different tradition. She was raised in an Episcopalian church but became, in her words, "kind of an atheist at age eight" but still felt a strong spiritual tie to the natural world. When she was in college, she spent a semester in India and studied in the home of Krishnamacharya, who at ninety-eight was known as the "father of modern yoga." His son taught yoga to Mari, which involved meditating, breathing, and separating herself from the frenzy of her own emotions in order to find the part of her that is calm and untouchable. It was the beginning of her own spiritual journey, but what had the greatest immediate impact was her daily elevator rides in the hotel where she lived. An older gentleman ran the elevator, and when he saw Mari, he bowed slightly and said, "Namaste."

That word is sometimes used in the West as a greeting, as if to say, "Hi, how are you?"

But that didn't seem to be how this man was using the word. Rather, Mari was struck by how deeply he looked at her when he said it. One day, she asked him what it meant.

"It means, 'The divine in me is greeting the divine in you.'"

So simple, yet to Mari, profound. As she later explained, "His whole life he brought people up and down an elevator, but the divine—that's how he saw himself and every person who came into that elevator, and it didn't matter if you were a prince or a pauper."

In time she went to massage school and learned cranial-sacral therapy. The therapist, she was told, is not an actual healer. The body can heal itself—it has its own wisdom—but sometimes it needs a little help.

Your cells are mostly water, so the body is its own ocean

of life, with its own rhythm that is imperceptible to the eye. That is the premise of cranialsacral therapy, which recognizes that spinal fluid surrounds the brain and fluctuates along the spinal cord, expanding and contracting, in a lilt that creates its own energy. That energy is detectable by touch. Mari volunteered at St. Francis Hospital in Hartford and discovered that even the most wounded bodies could be repaired. "If you're alive and breathing," she later said, "there is something healthy within you. I'm not looking for pathology. I'm putting my hands on your body and feeling for health. What is that health? It's the fluctuation of that fluid. I'm feeling that and connecting to it spiritually. That is the divine in the body. And it's guiding me to where you are a little stuck or constricted, and my hands just gently invite the body to open, and it's the body that creates the release inside."

In medical terms, that release is the body's nervous system returning to its parasympathetic state. In practical terms, for me, it offered an escape from my pain.

Once I was on the table, Mari asked me to slowly release my breath, and she began her light massage. In time I felt something in me relax, an ebbing, something positive. The session lasted an hour, though it felt as if I had entered some place unmoored from my own reality. We agreed to do four more sessions, and with each one, my body began to discharge pain. The relief would last only a couple of days, but that was a greater respite than anything else I had received. Thus began my Thursdays with Mari. I would continue experimenting with allopathic therapies, but I was now open to other approaches, and by the end of 2005, eighteen months after I had my first session with Mari, I was off most of my pain meds . . . and I also knew I was on a very different road.

I had a perception of who I was before I got hurt. Now

that was gone, and I had a choice. I could try to reassemble my component parts into something functional, or I could give up, become a drug addict, and die of an overdose.

What does success really look like? Well, it isn't always pretty, but it is a very personal journey.

It's about staying on course, no matter how powerful the gusts.

It's about fighting despair, accepting who you are, and then identifying a mission that will lift others around you.

It's about choosing which road you want to take.

I chose life.

6

MINDFUL LEADERSHIP BY LOSING ATTACHMENTS

JUST BECAUSE I CHOSE TO GET BACK UP DIDN'T MEAN I was going to get my career back on track. I had some basic things to figure out.

The trauma made me realize that life is measured by our attachments. We're attached to our job titles and our office responsibilities. We're attached to our house, our car, and possessions. For the most part, we go through life trying to amass more or better attachments as measures of our worth. That's not true of all attachments, of course, such as to our faith or our family.

But as leaders, I've come to believe that what we are most attached to is the image of ourselves.

How do we look and act? How do we carry ourselves? What's our vibe? There is a narcissism to the role, a self-absorption that can be channeled for good or ill.

In my case, because I was once athletic and had a rugged look, I was sometimes told, "You look like you'll be a CEO someday" or even that I was "right out of central casting." I had that aura, and I didn't mind that at all. To have a physical presence, I thought, was advantageous in any business setting. I wanted to be imposing, even intimidating. That's how I was brought up. That's how you win. But sometimes I was too headstrong, too impatient for my own good.

That was certainly true in the early days of my career.

After I received my MBA from Cornell in 1984, I had an interview with Drexel Burnham to work with Michael Milken, and I might have gone there, but a friend called and asked if I wanted to join him in starting an HMO. "What's an HMO?" I asked. The start-up was called SelectCare. There were five of us, all just out of college, in a 1,500-square-foot office. But the guy who was supposed to know how to operate the business didn't know how to operate it at all. In SelectCare's third year, it ran out of money, and the person who was nominally in charge left. The board named me as head of operations and marketing, which I thought was amazing, given that I was only thirty-one.

I pulled out one of my textbooks from Cornell and devised a new operations and marketing plan. But creating a plan on paper is one thing. Implementing it is something else. Our main problem was that we were moving too fast. We couldn't keep up on our claims, we were getting sued by hospitals and doctors, and even doing the basics—like getting ID cards to customers on time—was a chore. I hired an executive from Blue Cross Blue Shield, but progress was slow. One day I received a call from a client who complained about the damn cards, so I walked down the hall and entered the woman's office. She was meeting with her team.

I absolutely lit into them. "I've got another client on the phone! It's screwed up again! I should fire you all and get a new group of people!"

I spun around and headed back down the hall. I was halfway to my office when a hand reached up on my back and turned me around. It was the woman I had just hired. "You know what," she said. "I know the ID card process is screwed up, and I can actually fix it. I've spent most of the morning working with these people to get their heads right on how to do it, and you just destroyed all that. So, you've got two choices. You can go back into that room and apologize for being an asshole and work with us, or I'm going to quit, and you're screwed. Which one will it be?"

I went into the room, apologized, and promised I'd learn more about the ID card process.

In addition to fixing our customer service operations, we devised a turnaround plan that involved outpricing, outmarketing, and out-hustling our much larger competitor, Blue Cross Blue Shield of Michigan. I was ultimately promoted to president and chief operating officer, and by the time SelectCare was restructured in 1994, it had $1 billion in annual claims paid and had 500,000 covered lives.

The experience taught me lessons about my own accountability, and it was an early realization that the mantle of leadership creates a burden that is greater than any reward you'll receive. But it didn't change my management style. I was relentless, and rather mechanical, in pursuit of whatever goal we were trying to achieve.

After SelectCare, I thought I would take some time off. We were living outside Detroit, in Rochester Hills, and I got a call from a recruiter for Sy Sternberg, who was running the group business at New York Life Insurance. (Group business is anything related to employers.) New York Life had bought a bunch of managed-care companies, similar to SelectCare, and Sy asked me if I would help rationalize the group business in preparation to either sell it or take it public.

I said no. I didn't want to work for a big insurer, and I didn't want to move to New York. Plus, I was having too much fun in Michigan without the responsibilities of a job.

The recruiter called me back and said, "You tell me how much you need to get paid to make Sy say, 'No.'"

So, Susan and I sat down and did that, and then we added 20 percent, and I sent him the number.

The recruiter called me back: "You're hired."

I wasn't expecting that, but now I had to go. I lived in a hotel in New York for six months, until Susan and the kids could join me (and we bought a house in Franklin Lakes, New Jersey). At New York Life, we created a subsidiary, NYL-Care Health Plans, for the group business, and I went about shutting down some units, selling off others, and improving operations overall. There was a lot of bloat, and it was my responsibility to eliminate it. I had to lay off employees or, in some cases, dismiss them because of performance. Everyone was on notice. When I would walk down the halls, I would sometimes say, "Heads on pikes," meaning, if something goes wrong, whose head do I put on a pike? Some of my colleagues had Darth Vader dolls that reproduced the villain's voice and theme song, and those colleagues would jokingly play those as I passed by.

I can't say I loved the Darth Vader comparison, but if it got their attention, it served its purpose. And our efforts succeeded. We achieved our operational goals, and in 1998, Aetna acquired NYLCare Health Plans for $1 billion in cash plus an earn-out.

I had no reason to doubt the value of my bare-knuckle management style. But once I had my ski accident, the physical part of my persona—the intimidating part—vanished. My neck wasn't straight, my shoulder was crooked, and my left arm had weakened, atrophied, and hung to my side, with limited motion. Now I'd only be "right out of central casting" if they were casting for someone whose injuries hadn't healed properly.

Overnight, my entire self-image was gone, that swaggering aura only a memory. It was if I got kicked in the teeth and I spit out all of my narcissism. Which may not have been a bad thing, except I also lost my confidence. I could no longer walk into a room and command respect. I had to reinvent myself, and the physical reinvention was only part of it.

I STILL EXPERIENCED a burning pain in my arm, but thanks to the cranialsacral therapy, I could at least begin the healing process. Initially, after my injury, my world was small. Could I sit up straight? Could I lie down? Could I put on a shirt or tie a shoe or hold a phone, and could I do any of this without pain? And when is my next pill? After I got off the pain meds (which would not come until 2006), my left arm still hung lifeless at my side, still bent at the elbow. But I was at least clear-headed, and I was able to master many of the basics, such as how to dress myself. I began to wonder what part of my old life I could recapture.

It turns out, a good deal. I figured out ways to once again ride a bike as well as a motorcycle—I rode the former through Europe for fourteen days, covering 1,200 miles. Both the bike and the motorcycle were built with custom handlebars, brakes, seats, and other accommodations. I could no longer take my dog to the river and go fly-fishing by myself. But if I took someone else, and I could tie my line in a new way, I could still fish.

Life was now a series of reinventions, but some parts of my life could not be reinvented. Playing the piano was one of them.

I took lessons as a kid, and I played Beethoven and Mozart

but had the most fun when I was a bit older and played at a neighborhood bar. I smoked my cigarettes and got free long-neck Budweisers, and I told the patrons to give me any subject and I'd tell them a joke (even the lame ones drew sympathetic chuckles). But mainly I ran my fingers across the keys, playing show tunes or top 40 hits or whatever crinkled sheet music was on the rack. There are piano players and there are pianists. Piano players play a song on the piano, but a pianist sits and becomes part of the piano. It's a relationship, a gestalt, something that transcends the properties of the instrument and elevates the music to another level. And in those loud, smoky dens of my youth, that's how I felt, and who I was.

I continued playing when I got married and after the kids were born; when I was stressed, I would sit at the keys and play for two hours straight. I played mostly classical or show tunes, though sometimes Lauren would leave behind a Billy Joel song. After my injury, I stopped playing and didn't even think about it, until about three years had passed and I happened to notice the grand piano in the living room. I was healthier now, so I took my seat on the bench. I could still play right-handed, but all of the one-handed compositions are for the left hand. The right-handed stuff was pretty simple, and it wasn't for me.

I had been a *pianist*.

But I could never be that again.

Now I can only dream about playing the piano, or lifting 360 pounds, or running—and I do have those dreams where I run through the fields, run through time, all so effortlessly. And when I wake up, the pain that I feel is the knowledge that I will never be what I once was.

My injuries benefited other relationships, however, particularly with my daughter. My all-consuming desire to win in business had come at a cost. I traveled a great deal, sacrificing time at home, missing the kids' games or events at school. But even when I was at home, I wasn't as attentive as I should have been. In Lauren's case, too often I would be driving her somewhere, but I would be on my phone in the midst of a conference call. Or over the dinner table, I would give her math problems or ask her questions like "If you were stranded on an island with only one type of animal, what animal would that be?" I thought these questions were fun and challenging, but they didn't really connect us emotionally. (Lauren's answer, by the way, was cows, which could provide food, milk, shelter, and tools, and they could be carved out and used as canoes.)

Like many fathers and daughters, we had our moments during her teenage years. I once grounded Lauren after she broke a promise about not attending a certain party where alcohol was served. I told her she couldn't go anywhere for the next couple of weeks unless I took her. She slammed her door and went to bed crying. In the morning, I found that Lauren had tacked a two-page letter to my bedroom double door, just like Martin Luther, telling me what an idiot I was. I had to admire her spunk.

Fortunately, things improved once I began to reorder my priorities in life. When Lauren was a student at Syracuse University, I would ride my Harley up to see her, she'd hop on the bike, and we'd drive around town. I just tried to be present, in every possible way, and form a genuine bond. We finally talked at length, four or five years after the fact, about the ski accident and what had actually happened on the mountain. Lauren told me that her grandmother blamed her for my fall; that somehow, she, Lauren, had distracted me while I was skiing on dangerous terrain and that she had been responsible for my suffering. I assured Lauren that she was *not* at fault—nobody was to blame, every skier falls, it was a freak accident.

I also said to her: "You're my daughter. Had I died making sure that you were okay, it would have been worth it."

WHILE MY INJURIES led to many changes in my life, what changed the least—at the outset—was how I conducted myself at the office. I felt as if I no longer had that leadership aura, but I hadn't really adjusted to this new reality. I continued to plow ahead, as always, trying to do what I thought was in the best interest of the organization, but that didn't work with everyone. Aetna did a lot of "360s," in which your peers and subordinates evaluate you, and I kept hearing that I lacked "empathy," was "too brusque," was too much of a "fighter," and didn't "give people a chance." Alternatively, I was also told that I was too informal and shared too much of myself with others.

Aetna hired a personal management coach for me, and he reiterated many of those same messages. Frustrated, I sent him an email that said these people didn't know what I had been through. I had to fight for everything I had in life, I came from nothing, I'm now dealing with a broken neck and chronic pain, and I wasn't going to let niceties interfere with what I thought was best for the company.

The coach called me back. "Look," he said. "I love you. You're fun to be with. You're really smart. And this company needs you to fix certain things if you're going to run it, and I know you will fix them. And if you don't, you'll run another company, and you'll be successful wherever you go. But I can't help you anymore. I'm no longer your coach."

And he hung up. *Damn,* I thought. *My coach just fired me.* I clearly had more to work on.

WHILE MY CRANIALSACRAL THERAPY sessions provided relief, I was still searching for something permanent to eliminate the pain. In 2006, two years after my accident, I tried a radical treatment with the drug ketamine hydrochloride. It was used long ago as a potent anesthetic, and it's still used for that purpose on horses. It is also a dangerous street drug, known as "Special K," and has been compared to crack cocaine. But it hasn't lost its therapeutic function. German doctors use the drug in high doses to induce coma in order to reboot the central nervous system so that the patient does not recognize existing pain. The FDA allowed ketamine to be used therapeutically as well, but in lower doses compared to those in Germany. I went to a hospital in Philadelphia to try it. After three days I began hallucinating. Then, on the fourth, I woke up stone-cold sober. My body had adjusted to the ketamine, and the doctors couldn't get me high enough, so they sent me home.

The drug made some impact—I was pain free for a month. But then the pain came back worse than before. I returned to the Philadelphia hospital, where every other Friday I received "boosters" of this drug—enough to cause hallucinations and perhaps to ease my pain. I did this for a couple months, and one day I was sitting in the infusion room, watching TV, and Rachael Ray came on. She was making a flaming mushroom ragout. I had on my headphones, listening to music, and just as she lit the dish, "Burning Down the House" played, and I was suddenly thinking: *Here I am, an executive of a major corporation, sitting here getting high on Special K, watching Rachael Ray making flaming mushroom ragout, and listening to "Burning Down the House." This has got to stop.*

Stress in my marriage only complicated matters.

Ours had been a loving and durable partnership, going back to our days in Detroit. Susan and I had attended nearby high schools, though she was two years younger than I and moved in completely different circles. I once saw her at a disco. She was five foot seven, had long dark hair, wore a jumpsuit, and was dancing with the John Travolta of our class. I stood there in my tank top, jeans, sandals, and a huge 'fro . . . and figured I never had a chance.

But we both ended up at Wayne State (for me, on my second time through), and we were part of a carpool with several other kids from our town. One day when she was dropped at her house, she asked me to walk her to the door. I did, and then she asked me to a Sadie Hawkins dance.

"Am I the fourth or fifth guy you've asked?"

"No," she said, "you're only the second."

We dated for a year. Like my family, Susan's didn't have much money—she made her own clothes—and because we both lived at home, we had to circumvent the watchful eyes of our parents. On St. Patrick's Day in 1978, a Friday, we were sitting at Gilbert's Lodge drinking green beer; I was going to drop her off and leave for the weekend with my friends, but I knew there was something I needed to do.

"We're spending a lot of time together," I told Susan, "and we should think about making this permanent. We should get married."

"I'm thinking you should ask my father," she said.

"Okay."

"But you've had three green beers, so why don't you come by Monday and do it properly."

Her father, Jim, was a career gunnery sergeant in the Marines who was once stationed at the White House. He was a large, intimidating guy who liked to smoke, drink beer, and work on his car. I thought I would ask for Susan's hand in a rather indirect way.

"So, what kind of food would you like at your daughter's wedding?" I asked.

"Why, are you a caterer?"

"No, I want to marry her!"

He thought about it briefly and then said, "If you take good care of her, great. And if not, I'll break your neck."

Susan and I got married the following year, and Jim and I had a great friendship over the years.

Susan was a wonderful partner, and we made a good team—when I went to Cornell, Susan earned ten dollars an hour as a hospital nurse to help put me through graduate school. We started a family, tried to raise our kids the right way, and maintained a strong bond. That was tested when Eric was diagnosed with cancer, but the entire family received the counseling it needed, and we remained unified.

Eric's trauma, of course, was immediately followed by my ski injuries, and my relationship with Susan could not withstand that stress. To cope, I was drinking and had stopped exercising, and my weight ballooned to 235 pounds from 185. I was angry. I was in pain. I was suicidal. And Susan and I were increasingly losing patience with each other. In June 2006, Susan and I took the kids to Italy to celebrate my fiftieth birthday, with visits to Milan, Florence, and Lake Como. It should have been a great trip, but nothing felt right, and one night in our hotel room, I told Susan, "This isn't working. I'm not feeling good. I want to have fun here, but I don't know if I want to stay. I want to go home."

She'd had enough. She said I was drunk all the time, I wasn't the person she'd married, and if I didn't get my act together, she didn't want to be married anymore.

That got my attention. I thought I was the one in the family who always had his act together. But that wasn't true anymore. Susan was right, and I knew I had to change. I stopped drinking, and I got rid of my final pain meds, ripping off the fentanyl patches that had been attached to my butt. I stopped complaining about my arm, got on an Exercycle, and started losing weight. My neck started straightening out, and my eyes became clearer.

I was still a fraction of the person I used to be, though I knew where to get help.

Beyond the cranialsacral therapy, Mari had been teaching me breathing techniques that would allow me to get through my day when my pain flared up. It was a natural way to self-medicate. She explained that breathing was part of the much broader practice of yoga, and she told me that yoga was what I really needed to do.

"That's for girls," I told her.

"One session," she said, "and I'll shut up."

To Mari, my problem was that my doctors were treating me as if I were fragile, too timid to be challenged. They couldn't see past the pharmaceuticals, and I had been on a fool's errand, placing my faith in drugs and other therapies that too often represent Western hubris or negligence, opioids being the most damning recent example. That was, Mari concluded, the absolute worst approach for me. Beyond the fact that the drugs worsened my condition, Mari knew, as she later said, that I was a "bad-ass"—someone who thrived on competition and conflict, someone who only felt alive if I was pushing myself to the edge. Mari didn't see me as broken or fragile, and she figured there was one way to convince me of the same. She was going to kick my ass.

She would do this in our yoga session, for which she prepared without using her left arm so she knew exactly what I was experiencing. It was all about stretching muscles and putting pressure on them, doing isometrics, pushing and yielding, pressing and holding, again and again, until my face glistened with sweat and my muscles burned and my limbs ached and the endorphins began to kick in and I was ready to scream, *Okay, dammit! It's not for girls!*

I was so sore the next day, I couldn't move, and I couldn't remember the last time I felt so good. I called Mari in tears. I knew what it meant to be alive again.

In search of greater understanding, I found Leonard Perlmutter's *The Heart and Science of Yoga*, which spelled out the eight steps of yoga science. I was fascinated by the integration of Western science and Eastern philosophy, and I began an inward journey to include these elements into my own life, with tangible results. I bought a Tibetan singing bowl, made of gold and bronze, which emits a range of sounds to restore normal frequencies, or vibrations, in the mind and body. It is called an om bowl because of its resonance. Meditation itself is about the search for peace, but it requires a step-by-step process to focus the mind, to screen out the noise of the senses until you enter a timeless state. It allows you to lose attachments—in my case, the attachment to my neuropathic left arm. Thus, my chant:

I have a body. I'm aware of my body. I'm not my body.
I have a mind. I'm aware of my mind. I'm not my mind.
I have thoughts. I'm aware of my thoughts. I'm not my
*   thoughts.*
I have desires. I'm aware of my desires. I'm not my desires.
I have emotions. I'm aware of my emotions. I'm not my
*   emotions.*
I have pain. I'm aware of my pain. I'm not my pain.

At the office, often during meetings, the pain would still roll through my body, and I'd look down. People thought I was zoning out. But I was doing my chant, until relief came.

Relief did not come to my personal life. Susan and I were in marriage counseling in 2008, and she was angry at what I'd put her through and demanded that I ask for forgiveness. I walked out of the room and cooled off, and when I returned, she said, "You've made enough money. It's time for us to have fun. We don't need to do this anymore. If you value your marriage, you'll give up your career. And if you don't give up your career, I don't want to be married to you."

"Don't make me make that decision," I told her, "because you won't like the answer."

Susan was correct on one point. We didn't need the money. After my ski accident, I had a letter for long-term disability, which meant I could have sat at home and received half of my current salary for the rest of my life. But if anything, I was even more ambitious now, not for personal gain but for the opportunity to do meaningful things in the world. I felt I was on a mission, and that mission was just getting started.

Susan and I had reached a point where we just wanted different things in our lives, and those ambitions, after three decades together, could not be reconciled. We separated and filed for divorce, concluding that our relationship had become, strictly speaking, unhealthy, not only for us but also for our children. But unlike many divorces involving corporate executives, this one was amicable and without fanfare. We avoided the lawyers and hired an arbitrator to help us divide the assets. When we had to see a judge to finalize the agreement, I picked up Susan and took her to the courthouse, and I held her hand as we walked to the table, where we sat down next to each other.

"Are you her lawyer?" the judge asked me.

"No," I said. "I'm her soon-to-be ex-husband."

"Why are you sitting there?"

"Well, I still love her, but it's not working anymore."

"Where's your lawyer?"

I told her that our arbitrator was sitting right there.

The judge made me read the settlement aloud, and then she asked Susan if she approved it. Susan said yes, and that was that.

I drove Susan to a friend's house. We had a glass of wine and said good-bye. We have remained strong partners in raising our children ever since, and I couldn't have been happier for Susan when she remarried several years later.

UNTIL SUSAN AND I separated, I hadn't shared much of my life, personal or professional, with Mari. I'd been seeking treatment from her for four years, and most of our sessions occurred with little verbal communication. But once Susan and I were separated, I let down my guard. I told her about the impending divorce, and I could feel the ice begin to crack. And then, on her birthday, I showed up with a dozen roses.

Mari seemed appreciative but then broke the news to me: "You're fired."

She explained that she could not have any kind of a personal relationship with a client.

"No, no, no!" I was practically pleading. "I need my cranialsacral therapy!"

She kicked me out and said a couple of months would have to pass before she saw me.

WHEN MARI AND I reconnected in late 2008, I was no longer her client but her partner. We're definitely a study in contrasts—I lived in a mansion, she lived in a small, sparsely furnished house. I drove a Bentley, immaculately washed and shined; she drove a Subaru Outback, with one headlight and a dent, and it got washed by God when it rained. I've worked in corporate America my whole life. She once worked on an organic farm in California and was paid each Friday with bushel of vegetables. I live big. She likes to say, "I live simply so others can simply live."

But her disdain for material possessions, for the trappings of success, was part of her appeal. I grew up poor and came to believe that if I only had money, that would be the answer to everything. Well, I climbed the ladder and I made the money. But it didn't spare Eric from cancer. It didn't fix my arm. It didn't save my marriage. It didn't make the world a better place. And when I was honest with myself, it didn't make me happy.

But my eyes were now opening. In Hindu teachings, *satchitananda* means "I exist, I am knowing, and in bliss." That state occurs when you lose attachments, and part of my own journey, as both a disabled person and a leader, was learning to do just that.

I had to lose the attachment to my persona and recognize

that I could no longer walk into a room and dominate the space.

I had to lose the attachment to the certainty of my own ideas. I had to put aside my belief that I was the smartest guy in the room.

I had to lose the attachment to the very idea of what success was or what happiness meant.

Mindful leadership is about listening, learning, and adapting. I would have to do better on all those fronts if I were ever to achieve something truly meaningful.

1

TRUST BEGETS TRUST

WALK INTO THE WHOLE FOODS IN NEW YORK ON COLUM-
bus Avenue near Ninety-eighth Street, and then travel due
north about twenty blocks and walk into a bodega. Both of
these stores are thriving, and they both sell food. But they
offer completely different items. On the Upper West Side,
you'll find Chesapeake shrimp salad, vegan Thai chili tofu,
and organic carrot juice. In Harlem, you'll see chips, snack
cakes, and quarter waters. The difference, of course, is that
these stores cater to two different populations. In the intensely
heterogeneous swirl of New York, adjacent neighborhoods,
and even adjacent streets, have their own preferences and pal-
ates, and to succeed, vendors have to cater to those desires.

Welcome to America.

That kind of diversity increasingly reflects the country in
which we live, and these fragmented markets have changed
the decision making of businesses. The top-down, central-
ized approach doesn't really fit this world, and that model
was probably never the best anyway. But CEOs embraced it
because it consolidated their authority. The median tenure
of CEOs at large companies is only five years, according to
Equilar, a research firm. The short time frame, in my view,
means that CEOs are even more nervous about any blunder
that could torpedo the stock, damage their career, or ruin

their legacy. To minimize that risk, they tend to centralize big decisions in the corporate headquarters and tread carefully until their tenure has expired.

But that approach is too insulated as well as too timid. Neither I nor any other executive truly understands the nuances of distant markets. Nestled comfortably in our wood-paneled offices, we may not even understand the nuances of our own market. We're simply too far removed.

The response, for leaders, is self-evident but profoundly difficult: Push decision making down into the ranks. Surrender some authority. Even if you're a global company, act locally by giving your managers agency. And finally, trust your employees. Trust them to think big, make mistakes, and take your company where it's never been. And if you can't trust your employees, your company is probably going to fail anyway.

MY THINKING ON this issue has been influenced by Dov Seidman, the author of the bestselling *How: Why HOW We Do Anything Means Everything* and CEO of LRN, which helps companies and leaders build ethical cultures. Dov describes how the corporate world has been restructured, through greater transparency and interconnectedness, and what behavior changes are needed to win. What I found most compelling, in his book and in conversation, is Dov's views on trust.

"In the past," he wrote,

> [t]he more progressive [bosses] would implore their people to think outside the box, which in their minds was a compliment. In my mind, it's an insult. If you trusted people, you wouldn't put them in a box in the first place.

Dov described an illuminating study about the give-and-take of trust. A neurologist discovered that when individuals were either given trust or they extended trust to others, their pituitary glands released a feel-good hormone called oxytocin. This created a biological virtuous cycle. "When you trust someone," Dov wrote, "their brain responds by making more oxytocin, which allows them to trust you in return. Reciprocity—doing unto others as they do unto you—seems to be a biological function; trust begets trust."

I believe that to be true, and it's shaped my leadership of Aetna.

When I became CEO, we had 35 million members, with operations in every state in the Union and in more than thirty countries around the world. I said we weren't going to run everything out of Hartford, and we weren't going to review all the important decisions that were being carried out all over the company. Part of this had to do with basic efficiency—we were wasting too much time reviewing what everyone else was doing, which meant too much time in meetings. In 2008, I added up the number of workdays in which I had to attend at least one major internal meeting. It was 180 out of 200. We had a staff of 250 people who did nothing but put together PowerPoints. So, we set a goal for 70 percent less paper, 10 percent fewer meetings, and 50 percent fewer people attending meetings.

I told them, "You should only attend meetings where you're needed to make a decision, not to learn about the topic."

The real message: we trust you enough to go out and do your job, so do it.

Now when we have our monthly results meeting, we have fifteen people in the room. Previously, it would have been eighty.

We wanted to give managers in the field the authority to make adjustments on benefits, marketing, and pricing. As Aetna has evolved from a health insurance company to a health care company, we've put much greater emphasis on what's actually happening in communities that influence health—everything from food security to clean water to safe streets. Parts of Appalachia have been devastated by opioids, whose treatment we cover through Medicaid. Some retirement communities in Florida have high hospitalization rates, which we cover through Medicare Advantage. The needs of one city look nothing like the needs of another, and the only way we can design the right policies is by having people on the ground who understand what's going on. This is no different from the Whole Foods and the bodega: different products for different communities, but that can only be done if people who understand those communities are involved in making the decisions. It's all about going local. Even Starbucks, which for several decades relied on designers in Seattle to replicate their stores across the country and the world, finally decided that one template does not fit all markets. Starbucks moved some of its designers to other cities so they could incorporate distinctive community attributes into new stores. A new location on Canal Street in New Orleans, for example, features a brass-instrument chandelier.

In placing greater trust in executives or managers, I'm not suggesting that the inmates run the asylum. I get heavily involved on specific problems when I have to. Trust is essential, but so too are verification, controls, a strong senior team, and vigilance. I compare my job to scanning a heat map. I sit over this giant matrix, and I see squares that are luminous (exceeding expectations), squares that are pallid (meeting expectations), and squares that are . . . blowing up.

Many leaders respond by abandoning the bad squares, but I believe the opposite is true. Leaders should spend more time with the underperformers and, when it makes sense, allocate additional capital to fix them.

If you have a business unit or an initiative that is struggling, the easiest thing to do is cut off its money and stanch the red ink before it begins. That's fine. But if you believe in the trust model—and if you recognize that you're going to have to cede some control so your organization can reach new heights—sometimes you have to let senior executives or managers fail now in order to succeed down the road. The trigger for a leader's engagement should be the size of the business unit (how much is at stake) and the quality of the plan to solve it (how much can be gained).

SEVERAL YEARS INTO my tenure as CEO, some members of my senior team came to me with what they thought was a great idea for a self-funded product in the small group market. They talked to me about "attachment points" and "reinsurance levels" and other attributes that would make it a success. I told them, "I've seen this movie before. I've started a few of these, and I've blown them up myself. I don't think it's going to work."

They insisted it would, so I agreed to it. Every quarter, I asked them how it was going, and every quarter they said fine. But it was an illusion. The new product struggled, and we took a $40 million charge.

The top executive involved asked me, "How'd you know that would happen?"

"Because I've done it," I said.

"Why'd you let us do it?"

"Because you wanted to, and you need to learn for yourself. Now, how are you going to fix it?"

To its credit, the team developed an improved plan and created a newer version of the product, and it's now one of our best sellers.

Each year, we set aside about $300 million as a contingency for just those kinds of setbacks. That's part of the trust model. I know I can fix a problem in five minutes. It's not because I'm smarter. It's because I've been through it, but now the organization has to learn so other leaders can absorb the lessons and pass them on to the next generation.

It's not always the case that the strong businesses, or at least those with high potential, will ask for more resources. Remember the heat map. Supporting the positive initiatives is just as important as reviving the struggling ones. Medicare Advantage, which began during President George W. Bush's administration, allows Medicare recipients to buy a comprehensive plan with broader coverage. Aetna provides it, and one year I discovered we were slowing down our advertising budget because the enrollment period was coming to an end. I thought that could hurt our growth in future years, and I was confident we could do better.

I asked the executive in charge, "How much more do you need?"

"Three million dollars," she said.

"You have it."

"What?"

"You have it. Just show me how you're going to spend it."

She got the money, and Medicare Advantage continues to be one of our best products.

Sometimes you have to ask, "What do you need?" And when you get the answer, you say, "Here it is."

And then you have to trust that those resources will be used as planned while also verifying the course along the way.

THE TRUST MODEL is also about your frontline workers—about having faith in their critical thinking and giving them support to make decisions so they can respond quickly and efficiently to your customers. It's about believing that they will protect the assets of the company just as zealously as senior executives but giving them the authority to make a real difference in their daily work.

That's not the way most companies are run, and that's not the way Aetna was run even after I became CEO. The top-down model of authority is hard to break. The perceived risks of losing that authority are too great. I felt that way myself. I thought I was doing well in communicating and engaging with employees, but only after I attended a town hall meeting in early 2016, in Jacksonville, Florida, did I fully realize how our failure to trust our frontline workers was holding back the company. Customer service reps play a critical role in any organization because they are the first point of contact for customers. They are literally the face, or the voice, of the company, and how they respond to requests or complaints can define the entire customer experience.

It's not an easy job. In Aetna's case, our customer service reps might receive fifty or sixty calls a day from our members, typically complaints about being denied something important: a prior authorization, a pharmacy prescription, an out-of-network provider. Our reps were not always allowed to resolve the matter right there on the phone. Instead they had to reach out either to a manager or, more likely, to someone else in another part of the company; or sometimes they'd have to direct the caller back to that individual's employer. No matter the outcome, the process would take days or even weeks, and the customer might need the medication or the service right now; so even a positive outcome led to great frustration.

Our system had other problems. Even when our customer service reps were able to resolve problems on their own, they often needed more time on the phone with our members, but our compensation structure created perverse incentives to keep the calls short: our reps' "handle time" was supposed to be eight minutes, they were supposed to take so many calls a day, and they were allocated so many minutes to write up their notes after each call. Our reps were evaluated, and paid, in part on how well they met these goals.

This highly structured approach is typical for any organization that receives massive call volume. Aetna receives *20,000 calls per hour,* and we have between 12,000 and 15,000 reps answering those calls at any one time. In that environment, it's obvious why clear procedures and strict guidelines were essential—and why our reps had to "stay on script" and move through their calls as quickly as possible. It's also important to note how health insurers operate: customers pay for their products and services, through premiums, *before* they receive them, which potentially creates a perverse incentive to deny claims. As a result, all health insurers, including Aetna, train their customer service reps to be more like benefit administrators who adhere to the rules and approve claims accordingly.

We wanted to try something completely new, and it began with torpedoing the top-down model of authority and trusting our frontline workers to help our members. Our team in Jacksonville conceived and initiated the effort, writing a proposal that would give them more leeway to make decisions. Aetna has many divisions, or silos, and they are not as integrated as they could be. A big part of the reps' proposal was giving them flexibility to directly call other parts of the company—our experts in clinical care, pharmacy, eligibility, network providers—so they could get answers quickly and then respond to our members. The goal was to break through the company's invisible borders; thus, the name of the program: Service Without Borders.

Another part of the proposal was to allow our reps to use their own judgment in granting one-time exemptions for products or services that Aetna was not obliged to cover. We often receive calls from members who've had a claim denied because of a miscommunication or some other misunderstanding. Regardless of who's at fault, if we don't have coverage responsibility, our reps are supposed to follow the rules and deny the claim. But in Service Without Borders, the reps could determine on their own whether it was an honest mistake, in which case the rep can grant the exemption and pay the claim as well as educate the member. If the rep felt that the member was clearly wrong, he or she would still deny the claim.

When we brought this proposal to the senior team, we expected pushback, and we got it. It was too radical a departure from how we'd always done business. We were going to let our reps go off script and let them use their own critical thinking to make important financial decisions. That approach could—pick your metaphor—"give away the farm" or "open the floodgates."

I thought otherwise. For starters, even if we saw our costs increase by covering more claims, that could still make long-term business sense. We know that our most profitable customer is the customer we have today. Our next-most-profitable customer is the customer whom we persuade to buy more products and services from us. Finally, our least profitable customer is the new customer, because it costs a lot of money to bring that person in. So instead of antagonizing our existing customers, we should, with reason, be trying to meet their needs and secure their loyalty.

I also believed that our customer service reps would be good stewards of company assets. Our reps speak with our members all day long. They know who has legitimate claims. They know who's trying to rip us off. They are also in the best position to make a positive impact on a member's life. We get calls all the time from customers who go to the pharmacy for, say, a $4 antibiotic, and for whatever reason, the pharmacist tells them that they are not eligible for that drug. Regardless of eligibility, we should cover it, because no one is trying to steal a $4 antibiotic, and the last thing we want to do is lose that customer over so small an item. It's also much better to pay for that item now, or even a much more expensive product or service, than to receive a complaint from the member and then spend the resources on a protracted internal review process that may or may not result in our paying the claim anyway.

We moved forward with Service Without Borders, starting with a pilot program in Jacksonville. We began with twenty customer service reps, and then forty, and they had 500,000 customers and a budget. We told the reps, if the costs spiked beyond certain thresholds, they'd have to come back to us, and we could always kill the program.

What happened? Our reps figured it out themselves. They created a central operation so that when complaints came in and they didn't know the answer, they knew immediately where to call in the company to get the answer—they broke down the silos, calling it "phone a friend." They created support groups in the organization, which met on a daily basis to discuss tough cases—someone is admitted to the hospital, there's a huge bill, what's in-network, what's out-of-network, what gets covered, what doesn't?

Far from giving away the farm, the reps were more accountable with the money than we ever imagined, and after a year, they had spent less than 20 percent of their budget.

Trust begets trust, and that applies to every business and every industry.

Even more telling for us was that in our follow-up calls with members, we saw satisfaction scores increase by 10 percent. By placing trust in our reps, the dynamics of their conversations with members changed completely. We took the edge off. Whereas the mind-set of our reps had been typically "defend and protect," it was now "How can I help?"

This leads to another critical point. As the pilot program advanced, we discovered that it was a terrific service model, but we needed something more directional for our reps. They have more power, but to what end? What's the real purpose behind all this?

That led to our statement of a Common Purpose: *to advocate for our members' best health*. It had nothing to do with minimizing costs, maximizing profits, or increasing shareholder value. Instead, we wanted our reps to actively engage our members to determine if they were receiving all of their benefits and, if not, how we could make it happen. If a member made a mistake in believing that a product or service would be covered, we'd cover that claim and use it as an opportunity to educate the member on what benefits were available and how to maximize their benefits in the future. We were intentionally increasing our own short-term costs to promote the long-term health and well-being of our customers. This was an easy transition for our reps, because these were precisely the kinds of conversations that they had wanted to have for years! They could spend their time really listening to our members, building trust, and solving problems.

Here is what Service Without Borders means in practice: We often receive calls from a member who's standing with her child at a Walgreens pharmacy and the pharmacist tells her that her insurer won't cover some drug. So, she calls us and asks why this item isn't covered. Under our old system, our rep looks her up in the computer and regretfully informs her that she is not eligible, and she needs to speak with her employer to find out why.

Under our new program, our rep receives the same call but now puts her on hold and calls a colleague responsible for eligibility. That colleague calls the woman's employer, which checks the status of the stranded mom at Walgreens and discovers that she had been erroneously left off the eligibility list. Our Aetna team immediately downloads that information into the Walgreens files, and Walgreens fills the prescription while the woman is still on the phone with the customer service rep.

That's not a hypothetical. Those kinds of experiences happen all the time. To convey this new trust model, we gave our reps inverted organization charts to emphasize that the power lies not with the few executives, who now sit at the bottom, but with the many frontline employees, who are now at the top.

Another important lesson: just as you have to trust your employees, you have to trust your customers as well. Of the 20,000 calls we get each hour, maybe a hundred or so are from people who are trying to cheat us. Our defend-and-protect policy was geared to combating the dishonest 1 percent, not to making life better for the honest 99 percent. That doesn't make much sense. Besides, our reps are smart enough to identify most of the scofflaws. Even if we incur additional risks, we will save money in the long run by having our reps advocate early for our members' health, staving off costlier care down the road.

In 2017, we rolled out Service Without Borders across the company, and the training included videos on critical thinking, empathy, and other traits that will be helpful on the front lines.

While I wish we had introduced this program far earlier, I'm not sure it would have been possible twenty years ago or even ten years ago. That's because it relies heavily on communication technology in allowing our far-flung employees to immediately reach one another as well as to promptly contact providers, clients, distributors, and others. I also believe communication technology has changed the expectations of our members, as they no longer believe that traditional barriers of time and distance should impede service. They expect speed, efficiency, and precision in all their transactions, and that's what we as a business community need to deliver.

The old management model—in which you follow the rules, curb your individuality, and get your paycheck—no longer works. We don't have a talent problem in this country. We have a corporate culture problem that prizes obedience over creativity and repetition over fulfillment, and our workforce, particularly millennials, raised in the Digital Age, will no longer accept that. What they will accept is the trust model, and as Dov Seidman told me, "Trust is like love. You don't get it unless you give it."

My goal is to stand back and let the company work, and that's hard for operators like me. But I've reached the point where I'm ready to stop requiring many of the traditional oversight tasks, even reviewing expense reports. You send us your expense report, and we'll reimburse it, but if you're stealing from us, we'll dismiss you. I realize the trust model carries risks, and I'm not advocating throwing out all the safeguards. But I believe that most employees will do the right thing when given the chance.

Trust and verify.

And keep the faith.

8

PROMOTING VALUES

CORPORATE EXECUTIVES ARE MORE COMFORTABLE TALK-
ing about shareholder value than moral value, and that's un-
derstandable. Shareholder value is easy to measure. It's clean.
It doesn't invite controversy or dissension. But corporate
leadership should also be about other kinds of values: social
justice, codes of conduct, and what we believe in as individuals, companies, or communities. Mission-driven leadership
requires engagement at all levels of the organization—where
we live, work, and play.

Employees don't come to work for guidance on moral values, but I believe they look to their leaders for signals that go
beyond bottom-line results. I've tried to provide that leadership, in word and deed, in ways large and small.

When Congress passed a significant corporate tax cut
in 2017, some of America's most prominent companies announced one-time bonuses for employees. The announce-
ments drew big headlines, but I thought these bonuses
shamefully obscured the tax cut's true significance; namely, it
would trigger shareholder buybacks, which would dispropor-
tionately benefit wealthy investors while enriching corporate
executives whose compensation was tied to their companies'
share price. And sure enough, in the first quarter of 2018,
companies repurchased $178 billion of shares, up more than

42 percent from the same period in 2017 and representing the largest amount ever repurchased in one quarter, according to S&P Dow Jones Indices.

My feeling at Aetna was, let's use the tax cut to invest in our members—let's make their lives better—or if we do allocate any of the windfall to employees, let's make it sustainable as opposed to a one-time bonus. In short, we weren't going to succumb to the quick PR boost if the move didn't benefit our company long-term. That's who and what we are, and that's a value statement.

I also put our values front and center when I believe our company has been wronged or defrauded. In those instances, I instruct our lawyers to file a suit. Rarely is it about the money, as the potential financial rewards are usually minimal compared to the time, energy, and expense involved in any legal remedy. But I insist on it because it's about the principle. In 2012 Aetna sued a network of surgical centers in Northern California for a complex overbilling scheme that involved kickbacks to referring physicians. (During a three-year period, we alleged the centers billed us $23 million for procedures that should have cost us $3 million.) Those types of suits are very difficult to win, and this one took four years. But a California jury ruled in our favor and awarded us $37.4 million in damages. Given the size of our company, and after lawyer fees and expenses, that's a pittance, but the effort reflected our values. And the surgical centers went out of business.

I acknowledge that my approach can be uncompromising, and that includes personnel decisions. I can be unforgiving not just for obvious misdeeds, such as fraud or gross misconduct, but I am particularly unforgiving when someone fails to put the needs of our customers first, especially when that failure can threaten a customer's health or well-being. I can't think of a more important value than that.

Again, I like to hear directly from our members, so I ask to see their letters, emails, and social media posts. At one point, I was reading letters from patients who were not receiving their specialty medications. One letter explained how a member was not getting his long-acting psychotropic drug for schizophrenia. I forwarded the letter to the executive in charge of our pharmacy operations and told him I didn't think he was really in control of what was going on. I asked him when was the last time he'd been to our office in Orlando, which was responsible for our specialty pharmacy operations.

He told me it had been more than a year.

"You've got all these problems down there," I said, "and you haven't been there in over a year. Let's see who gets there first."

I was in Orlando the following week, on a previously scheduled trip, and I saw the executive was there. But few people knew him. He was walking around introducing himself. He told me that the pharmacy operations overall were doing very well—our costs were down, and fewer than 1 percent of our customers were "out of service," or without their meds.

But he didn't know how many people were without their specialty meds, which are prescribed for serious, often life-threatening, conditions.

I told him: "Anybody on a specialty med cannot be out of service, so there should be someone in your operation who wakes up each day with a list of people who are out of service, and that list should be tattooed to their forehead. And when they are walking around the office, they should be looking at that list and saying, 'What are we doing for John Smith today?' It's just unacceptable. Make sure that nobody is out of service."

I asked him to send me a report every Friday at noon with an update on the list of who's not receiving his or her specialty meds. And each Friday, for the next four weeks, he sent the report. But I didn't think I was getting all of the information that I needed. I was about to call the executive when I received a letter from a mother who said that her son almost died three years ago before he was diagnosed with severe schizophrenia, but thanks to Aetna, she got him on the right medicine, and he's been on it ever since. But all of a sudden, and without explanation, Aetna stopped covering it. Every day for the past several months, she wrote, she'd been fighting Aetna to resume coverage, she'd gotten nowhere, and she was afraid that her son could do something that was life threatening to himself or others.

I sent this letter to the pharmacy executive as well as to his boss and to our head of customer services and to our chief medical officer. I wanted to know what the hell was going on. After a flurry of calls, they discovered that the drug had been moved from one plan design to another, which meant a different department at Aetna was now responsible, and this customer had fallen through the cracks. It was a procedural error on our part, and it should have never happened.

I learned about this on a Friday evening, and at 9 p.m., I sent the pharmacy executive an email. I told him I wanted to see if in fact this young patient with schizophrenia was on his out-of-service list, and I wanted an explanation on how the problem was being handled, and I wanted that information by midnight. And if I didn't get it by midnight, I wanted him in my office personally at noon on Monday.

At 11:45 p.m., the executive sent me an email saying the boy was not on the list because they didn't think that schizophrenia was life threatening and they had not had time to compile the list for all out-of-service patients.

I emailed him back and told him here is how you compile the entire list. You go to each of your forty customer service reps and you ask them, "Who's out of service?" And you ask them why, and you write those names down, and you work that list every single day. You don't need anyone to write a report, you don't need anything else, you just do it. And, I wrote him, I wanted him in my office at noon on Monday.

When he came in, he looked like hell. "I've been nervous all weekend not knowing what's going to happen," he said.

"Now you know what that mother felt like," I said. "For three months, she worried about her son going into severe schizophrenia, maybe hurting himself, maybe hurting others. That's how it feels."

Sure, I was concerned about our corporate interests. If one of our customers died because of a procedural error, it would create massive liabilities. Everything that we have tried to build as a company could be jeopardized. But financial concerns were *secondary*. What made me livid was our role in putting that mother through months of anguish and the possibility that we were endangering her son. We were responsible. We were putting that boy's life at risk. We just didn't care enough to do the right thing.

I fired the executive on the spot. He didn't even report to me, which meant I had given his superiors more work. I communicated this specific example to our employees at subsequent town halls.

That's another way to send a very clear message about a company's values.

WHAT WE CARE about is also expressed in much more positive ways—our charitable contributions through the Aetna Foundation, for example, or the 400,000 volunteer hours from our employees each year. Tolerance and respect are highly prized as well, and I've been uniquely engaged on this front since 2006, when as president of Aetna I was made executive sponsor of diversity.

It was an odd position for a middle-aged white guy, but that was the point. Ron Williams wanted to challenge me. (Ron himself was Aetna's first African American CEO.) In my new role, I met with Aetna's various employee resource groups, including one that represented gay and lesbian employees, called ANGLE.

I asked them who their executive sponsor was.

They said they didn't have one.

I asked why not.

They said that all the other executives were afraid that they'd be accused of being gay.

Because I grew up poor and because our family was never accepted in elite circles, I always had an affinity for the underdog or anyone else who felt like an outcast. I'm sure people in my community held biases, but that didn't influence me or the people I hung out with. We just accepted others for who they were and didn't think that much about it, and I've lived my whole life that way.

I wasn't going to sit idly by after hearing that Aetna's gay and lesbian employees had been effectively stranded, so I told them that I would be their executive sponsor. This started rumors that I was gay or led some secret double life. One person even stopped me in the hall and said, "I didn't know you were gay." I found no reason to dignify such comments with a denial, and I didn't particularly care what other people thought of me. Besides, I was more interested in doing something positive.

I suggested to ANGLE that it needed a mission. Instead of representing the interests of gay and lesbian employees, it should help Aetna reach gay and lesbian customers. We worked with the Gay and Lesbian Medical Association so that our provider directory now identifies LGBT-aware physicians. We sponsored programs in the gay community related to alcohol abuse and domestic violence. I wasn't on a crusade. I just wanted to help make positive change. Word of our efforts spread, and one day I got a call from a representative of Martina Navratilova, who said that Out & Equal Workplace Advocates wanted to give me an award for being the health care leader of the year.

"Wow, great," I said. "Do I get to have dinner with Martina?"

"Yes, you do."

"Then I'll be there!"

At the awards ceremony in Washington, D.C., I sat at a table with Chance Mitchell and Justin Nelson, the two founders of the National Gay & Lesbian Chamber of Commerce. The Affordable Care Act was steamrolling toward a vote, and I asked Chance and Justin what they thought about it.

They said they hadn't really studied it and didn't know what impact it could have on those they represented.

I told them that they should know the impact, so let's set up a call and try to figure this out.

First call I got from them, they asked if I would be on their board of directors, even though they'd never had a straight person in that role. I told them it was time, and as a result, I became the first straight ally on its board. They asked me if I had any objections to the NGLCC making the announcement in my hometown newspaper. I said of course not. In conversations, Chance and Justin talked to me about gay rights and their efforts to advance them. I responded, "You're the Chamber of Commerce. Be relevant to that. You've got one of the highest-educated demographics in the country, and that could be a powerful force in the business world. How do we help that?"

We held a planning session with the board, and the idea emerged to persuade federal, state, and local governments to recognize gay- and lesbian-owned businesses as minority suppliers, which would help them get federal contracts. The NGLCC would be the certifying organization. And that's exactly what happened, and it was a huge benefit to those small businesses.

Rumors about me began to swirl again, this time in business and media circles, including at Gawker, the gossip website. As it happened, my daughter, Lauren, worked at Gawker. When the site published a critical story about me or Aetna, she texted me: "Sorry dad." When Gawker heard that I was on the board of the NGLCC, it decided it was going to "out" me as being gay. ("Outing" famous or successful people was one of Gawker's amusements.) The editor didn't know that Lauren was my daughter but thought we might be related, so he asked Lauren to confirm the story that Mark Bertolini was gay.

"But he's not gay," she told him.

"How do you know?"

"Because he's my father."

The story didn't go any further, but it didn't matter to me one way or the other. I was going to continue to support the values of diversity, inclusion, and equal rights. Not long after I became CEO, a highly publicized hate crime was committed against a gay man, and ANGLE asked me if the company would fly the rainbow gay-pride flag atop our headquarters. I said yes. We also fly that flag each October 11, which is Gay Pride Day, and I write a blog on the company website about the importance of respecting others' differences. Those blogs are well received, but not by everyone. One employee from Dallas wrote back on the blog, "You're going to hell because you're allowing this spawn of the devil to be rewarded. How dare you!"

I wrote a personal email to her: "You've got to have some tolerance for people."

She emailed me back: "Go f— yourself."

ON JUNE 12, 2016, Aetna had two employees who were murdered at the Pulse nightclub massacre in Orlando; the gunman killed forty-nine people in all. I was devastated. I called Chance and Justin on the Sunday of the shootings and asked what I could do to help. They suggested raising the gay-pride flag at our headquarters. We did that early Monday morning, and I tweeted the image of the flag over our building with the sun rising. When I got into my office, I had a voice mail from Connecticut governor Dannel Malloy as well as emails from the heads of the state house and senate. They all saw the flag, and they thanked me and the entire company for our support of the victims.

Then I looked out the window, and I saw the Cathedral of St. Joseph, an architectural wonder whose bell tower reaches 281 feet high and whose white concrete sides are sheathed with Alabama limestone. But something was different—the large center bronze doors were open. The doors themselves are stunning pieces of art: they include sculptured images of the canonization of St. Peter and of the Savior freeing St. Joseph from Limbo. It was the first time in ten years that the doors had been left open. I asked what was going on and was told that the church was keeping its doors open so that any Aetna employee could enter and pray. St. Joseph would also hold a mass for the shooting a month later. I thought it was an extraordinary act of grace that this cathedral for the Archdiocese of Hartford, where the local archbishop presides, was trying to heal a community in the aftermath of a massacre that specifically targeted gay men and women.

We were all trying to comfort each other, and the cathedral's open doors spoke to me in a very personal way.

I was an altar boy when I was growing up and considered going into the seminary. On my first day of Communion, I had a scapular and a cross put around my neck. I also had a rosary in my pocket, and whenever I was fearful, I would say a decade of the rosary. Each night I would read a passage from the Bible so that I would complete the entire text in one year. I attended Mass on a regular basis. I also stayed active as an adult, helping to found the Christian Family Movement in Hartford.

But when Eric was in the hospital, I read about the priests who were molesting children and who were then protected by the church—a failure not just of the men but of the institution. I sent a letter to Archbishop Cronin, who was at Fall River, serving New England, when the abuse occurred, and I asked how this could have happened. I received a nonresponsive letter in return, with "Love of Christ" at the bottom.

At that point I decided I was through with the institutional Catholic Church, and I stopped attending Mass and refused to even enter a place of worship. After my ski accident, the doctors cut off my scapular and cross, and when I got home, I burned them. I torched my rosary as well. I remained spiritual. I had not lost faith. But I no longer believed in the people who ran the church, and I had no intention of entering the Cathedral of St. Joseph.

Several months before the Pulse shooting, I received a letter from Rev. Leonard Blair, who had been appointed the archbishop of the archdiocese in Hartford in 2013. He asked to meet with me, and in our meeting, he was curious why he had not seen me at St. Joseph, which has a long history with Aetna. (After the cathedral was destroyed by fire in 1956, our auditorium was used for Mass for three years, and Aetna had long been a major donor to St. Joseph.) I told Archbishop Blair about my estrangement from the church. He apologized for the mistakes of the past, and he became emotional as he explained how he had spent many years trying to make things right, first in Toledo, Ohio, and now in Hartford.

It was a powerful conversation. I admired the archbishop. He was also from Detroit, and I thanked him for his words. But I said to him, "Please don't expect to see me sitting in your pews."

Then came the Pulse massacre, and the open bronze doors were a reminder that this was also a time for open hearts; a time for healing, unity, and forgiveness. So, on that day, I strode across Farmington Avenue, walked up the concrete steps, and entered the cathedral through the open doors, and there, amid the magnificent glass etchings that revealed the Savior present in the Gospel, I sat in a pew, bowed my head, and prayed.

9

A BLUEPRINT FOR RADICAL CAPITALISM

NEAR THE END OF THE WESTERN FILM *TOMBSTONE,* DOC Holliday (Val Kilmer) is lying on his deathbed, and Wyatt Earp (Kurt Russell) tells him, "All I ever wanted was to live a normal life."

Doc scolds him: "When will you wake up! . . . There is no normal life. There's only life. That's all. Just life."

When people ask me, "What is the right balance between home life and work life?" I want to scold them: "When will you wake up! There is no balance. There's only life."

I've come to this view in part from my experiences as a survivor of a spinal cord injury. I have chronic, burning neuropathic pain in my left arm, from my ear to my fingertips. For me to thrive at work, I have to do many things outside of work regarding my mental and physical health. I have to be rested. I have to be clearheaded. I have to resist the temptation of drugs and other false elixirs. There is no separation for me between my home life and my work life. It's just life.

In different ways and in different forms, I believe this blending of our lives is true for everyone. As employers, we cannot expect workers to walk into our doors, give us their full energy for the entire day, and then walk out—and pretend that what happens in the rest of their lives has no bearing on their performance. That's not realistic. Most large companies offer employee assistance programs, but those are reactive, intervening after problems have surfaced. There's a better way.

Corporate leaders talk all the time about "investing" in their employees, which typically implies financial assistance in improving job skills or taking college courses. Those investments are worthy, but I believe we need a broader, more humanistic approach, something that views workers beyond simply economic agents, something that invests in their emotional, spiritual, and physical needs. Let's be clear about what's at stake. First and foremost, we are trying to improve the health and well-being of our employees, and that alone is sufficient. But if we succeed, our employees will be far more motivated, productive, and inspired—which is exactly what our economy needs. We're investing not only in the well-being of our employees and the health of our companies but, I would submit, in our communities, families, and a new capitalist model.

MY RETHINKING OF this topic began at a refuge in the redwood groves of California, where Mari was taking classes at Mount Madonna.

She was immersed in not just the postures (*asanas*) and breathing (*pranayama*) but also Vedic chants, Yogic Philosophy, and more. I joined Mari on one of these trips in 2009, and the instructor, Gary Kraftsow, discovered what I did for a living and asked to speak with me. He wanted all of Aetna's employees to be given the opportunity to take yoga, with the company covering the costs. But Gary didn't understand my world, nor I his; so Mari served as translator. By the time I was CEO, I was in a position to introduce such a radical program, but I was skeptical. We needed empirical evidence. I told Gary that we should focus on one health benefit derived from yoga and try to prove it in a study, and if we could, we could then offer the program more broadly.

I asked him what that one benefit could be.

"Stress," he said.

Gary and Mari began developing a pilot program, while I had the much tougher job of convincing my senior team that we should offer yoga to employees. I made the case in a meeting, and afterward, our chief medical officer, Dr. Lonnie Reisman, was nominated to come into my office.

"Mark," he said, "we're not doing yoga. It's a stupid idea."

"Lonnie, it's not stupid, and the fact that I'm the CEO of this company with this huge disability, and I'm not taking drugs, is a perfect example of what yoga can do for people."

Lonnie resisted but was not obstinate, and eventually he agreed to a study. We recruited 239 volunteer employees from both the east and west coasts and divided them into three groups: one that did yoga, one that meditated, and a control group. We stratified participants by stress levels, measured by cortisol levels and heart-rate variability. (Our west coast employees, interestingly enough, were more stressed.) We asked participants to keep journals, including their sleep patterns, and we also looked at their medical costs over the previous two years.

The study lasted twelve weeks, with one group of participants taking yoga classes once a week while instructed to exercise at home. The results stunned the biostatisticians: the employees who did yoga or meditated experienced more than a 50 percent drop in stress levels. The participants also kept journals, which showed an increase in productivity, per employee, by sixty-nine minutes a month. We published our results in the *Journal of Occupational Health Psychology*, though Mari didn't find the results all that groundbreaking.

"We proved what yogis have known for five thousand years," she said.

The initial resistance we had to the program quickly disappeared. Importantly, we made the program all-volunteer, which itself is part of showing respect for others. If I had announced that everyone at the company had to follow yogic principles, I would have been scorned, and I also would have violated the entire spirit of Eastern philosophy. We've now had more than 18,000 employees go through the program (including, by the way, most of my senior staff). We knew, from our initial study, that employees who have the greatest stress (those in the top quintile) have $2,500 more in health care costs per year than employees with average stress. Anxiety causes your body to store fluids to protect it from whatever it thinks the assault will be. Your weight goes up. Your body resists insulin, causing type 2 diabetes. Your heart rate and blood pressure go up. Your vessels constrict. You don't sleep as well. It was obvious to us why higher-stressed employees increase health care costs and why programs to minimize stress were also good for the bottom line.

But that wasn't the most important part. We knew, based on the journal entries from our employees, that reducing stress improved marriages, repaired families, and even helped to save lives. Those messages hit home for me, as I knew what it was like to be overwhelmed by despair, I knew the limits of conventional therapy, and I knew that our yoga and meditation program, at nominal costs, had an ROI that could not be matched by any other investment.

These practices have another benefit that I believe is particularly relevant to the workplace. Yoga is about being "present in the moment," which is easily lost in the Digital Age and something we in corporate America, myself included, have to be aware of every day.

Being present in the moment means giving higher consideration to people than to tasks—at its core, it means taking care of one's self in order to take care of others. As a manager, it means delivering bad news early and in person. It means always assuming positive intent in what everybody does, and if you don't see that positive intent, you are required to find out what that person is trying to teach you that you don't yet understand.

It also means managing to people's energy, not their time. I often don't have end times to my meetings. When we're done, we're done, and if we end fifteen minutes earlier than expected, great. We don't have to torture one another with affirmation, and we can just go back to taking care of our customers.

Being present in the moment has lofty goals, and I don't always achieve them, but in striving for them, I bring my best self to work every day.

MARI'S INITIAL INVOLVEMENT was critical to this effort and a reminder that if you're going to have an impact as a corporate leader, you need workplace partners along the way. A workplace partner is someone who signs up for the journey, believes in what you're trying to accomplish, and will stand with you when you're under siege. You don't anoint a workplace partner. The relationship has to develop naturally, and you have to be open to it: Your partner has to be able to tell you when you're wrong or when you've gone too far or when you just need to shut up.

Like every CEO, I've had numerous workplace partners—I call Steven Kelmar, my chief of staff, my "work wife," because I rely so heavily upon him. But I found an unlikely workplace partner in Mari. She's my personal partner, of course, but she's also someone who previously held corporate America in low esteem. In retrospect, that may have been what made her so effective.

Mari taught some of the early yoga classes at Aetna, though no one knew about our relationship. She met some of the employees, who told her about the challenges in their life, both at work and home, and she shared those with me. She told me directly: "They can't make ends meet. They're not making enough money." She learned that health care costs too much and that some had enrolled their dependents in Medicaid while others were talking to loan collectors during their breaks or cashing out their retirement accounts to cover expenses. The journals that our employees kept for our yoga study confirmed what Mari had told me. These entries revealed how our workers were caring for children with disabilities or for parents at the end of life; how they were struggling to pay their monthly rent and stay clear of alcohol or drugs; or how they were trying to overcome a difficult divorce, isolation, or loneliness.

I knew that everyone had problems, but these messages—like distress signals from a ship—unnerved me. I had specifically tried *not* to be the executive who drives by the masses and offers little more than the queen's wave. I tried to be a visible leader, communicating on various platforms, doing town hall meetings. But I primarily focused on our corporate mission and what we were doing as a company. I needed to broaden the conversation.

I continued to conduct town hall meetings around the country, but afterward, I tried to really talk to our workers and ask them how they were doing and what was going on in their lives. Many of the responses centered on pocketbook issues, but the comment that had the biggest impact came from a woman who told me that she couldn't afford Aetna's health care.

Here I was, running what I thought was a really successful company, but my colleagues were having these kinds of struggles. Mari wouldn't let me forget it, either, and not just about Aetna employees. Sometimes we would be in a car and she'd point out the tumbledown homes or abandoned store fronts, and she'd say, "You run a big company. You make a lot of money, but are you really doing anything for anybody?"

I once told Mari, "You remind me of the person I used to be," and I knew I needed to get back to being that person.

For our own employees, I knew, at minimum, that we had to address the pocketbook issues. I also knew that the economic recovery was slow and uneven, and that companies were hoarding cash but not investing. Then, in 2013, I found Thomas Piketty's *Capital in the Twenty-First Century*, about income inequality and its threat to our social fabric. The book is dense and some of the charts inscrutable, but it scared the hell out of me. If we don't close the gap between the rich and poor, we're going to face social unrest for years to come, easily exploited by demagogues and charlatans. Piketty's analysis was supported by other academic papers. According to the economists Emmanuel Saez and Gabriel Zucman, the distribution gap in household wealth in the United States *decreased* from 1929 to 1978 but has continuously increased since then, and this is due almost entirely to the rise in the concentrated share of wealth among the top 0.1 percent of Americans—from 7 percent of all household wealth in 1979 to 22 percent in 2012.

The issue had become part of our political discourse, and I was talking to economists and policy experts who were describing measures to address our growing income inequality by changing laws: massive wealth redistribution through the federal government. I was skeptical. We had to act instead. So, I told my team that I wanted to know who our lowest-compensated employees were. How much do we pay them? What are their health care costs? Are they single? Married? With kids? What are their lives like? I wanted a complete data dump to find out if we could raise the wages of our lowest-paid workers.

And I waited, but I couldn't get what I needed from our human resources department. It's not that they were opposed to raising our minimum wage. They just didn't feel the urgency and really didn't get what was at stake. Maybe the very idea of intentionally increasing our labor costs was too alien to fully embrace. I tried to prepare my senior leaders by having them read Picketty's book—I gave it to them for Christmas—so they could better understand the threat.

We also needed partners outside Aetna to make the case for what we were trying to do. I sit on the board of the Peterson Institute for International Economics, a highly recognized research organization, and I told its president, Adam Posen, about my idea. He was stunned—in a positive way—that we would do something that seemed so counterintuitive: most CEOs want to lower wages. But Adam agreed with our objective, and I asked him if he and his team could draft some white papers or op-eds on the economic benefits of raising wages. He did, and his team's work helped influence the larger debate.

I finally got the internal data at Aetna that I needed, and I learned that among our minimum-wage employees, 80 percent were women, most of them single mothers, some on food stamps, some on Medicaid. I told my head of HR that our profits are going up, our P/E ratio is going up, or share price is going up, we're on this great ride, but all these people are being left behind. What are we going to do about it?

She said, "Let's give them a fifty-cent raise."

"Wait a second," I said. "How much is that?"

"It's like $3 million."

"That's nothing."

After our third meeting, I finally said to her, "Do you even care about these people? Why do I have to push?"

I said we should raise the wage to $16 an hour from $12.50. "Tell me why that doesn't work," I said.

I was applying the same principle that we used with our introduction of yoga and meditation: if our company was to grow and prosper, we had to invest in our employees. We could have the best products in the world, but if our frontline workers are not engaged and motivated, we lose.

I still faced resistance on raising the minimum wage, from my HR head and others. They told me that we'd be paying above-market rates, particularly in states with lower-than-average wages. We'd be hurting our bottom line. We have shareholders to serve. We have Wall Street to satisfy. We just introduced yoga. How fast can we go?

My head of benefits understood what I was trying to do, and she noted that the higher wages, if we paid them, would mean that those employees would lose certain benefits from the company or the government. She said let's look at our health benefits and try to lower those costs for employees. The result was a proposal to reduce out-of-pocket health care costs for those employees who were under 300 percent of the federal poverty line, and this gave many of them our richest benefit plan at the price of our least rich plan.

When we took these ideas to our senior leaders, the first question was, "What will the hard savings be?"

That question raised the specter of management by spreadsheet, which, as I've noted, doesn't speak to our values.

I told my team, "If that's the question"—what are the hard savings?—"we'll never get an answer that we like."

I suggested that we move beyond traditional spreadsheet analysis and include soft benefits, or those that are more difficult to quantify. So, we calculated the projected hard savings—lower turnover, lower training costs, higher productivity—that we thought were assured. Then we included probability-weighted soft savings (counting them as less impactful), such as greater engagement, increased camaraderie, and higher morale.

We determined that a raise to $16 per hour would cost us $10.5 million per year. Our accepted figure for turnover cost was $27 million per year, but that was only voluntary turnover. I asked for total turnover costs. How many people leave involuntarily? How much does it cost to hire their replacements? How long does it take to hire their replacements? How long does it take to train the new recruits? We looked at absenteeism, rework, productivity, dissatisfied employees, and our so-called net promoter scores, or surveys of new employees. (Our industry's general net promoter scores are below those of airlines and cable TV companies.)

We figured that our total turnover costs were $120 million per year. By that measure, the $10.5 million for increasing the minimum wage looked like a low-risk investment.

The process took two years, and I ended up replacing my head of HR, but significant change is never easy. To make the announcement, I went down to our largest call center in Jacksonville. We had to rent a hotel ballroom, and everyone was wondering why we were there. Rumors swirled that I was retiring. I had given an interview to the *Wall Street Journal* a week in advance but had embargoed the story until that night. I wanted the employees to hear about it directly from me. We had also given our top three hundred managers a heads-up the day before. We got them on the phone, and they said things like "This is the proudest moment I've had in forty-two years at the company."

Then I made the announcement, and the place erupted. I knew people would be happy, but I wasn't ready for the raw emotion. The tangible benefits were clear. The program affected about 7,000 employees, and many of them saw their wages increase by 33 percent and their personal disposable income increase by 45 percent. But the reaction reflected something deeper. Some people were crying; others were thanking the Lord because their prayers had been answered. I think many were in shock because it's not the sort of thing that companies do, and I believe that—beyond the financial benefits—our employees were gratified that their hard work was appreciated and their economic struggles were understood. In short, the company cared.

We heard from some dissenting voices as well. Employees who were already making $16 to $20 an hour wanted to know why they weren't getting a raise also. They had a fair point, but we said we were helping the people who were most in need.

I learned a couple of things along the way. To implement major change, I had to stay closely involved, not only to ensure that the initiative was progressing but also to signal that this was a top priority. I also had to secure the buy-in of my senior executives, as it would fall on them to carry out the changes (and those executives who didn't support the effort would no longer be part of the team).

I also needed the support of our shareholders. It's their money that we're spending. A few days after the *Wall Street Journal* disclosed the program of our investment in our employees, I was at a national investor conference and was meeting with our shareholders who represented the majority of our total shares. They were largely supportive, particularly once they understood the direct financial costs versus the benefits in employee retention, productivity, and satisfaction. This wasn't the first time I had spoken to them about the priority of long-term investments, nor the last.

Our wage increases and health care subsidies cost us about $20 million per year, and we haven't missed a beat in our performance.

The outside world saw our minimum wage increase as historic: *Strategy + Business* magazine wrote: "It was arguably the most visible wage hike by a chief executive since 1914, when Henry Ford doubled his assembly line workers' pay to $5 a day."

Since we raised our minimum wage, Walmart has raised its minimum wage for 1.1 million employees in the United States. So too have Amazon, Target, McDonald's, Starbucks, JPMorgan Chase, IKEA, Costco, and others. None of these moves triggered an inflationary spiral—a common if misguided argument against increasing low wages. But the idea of sharing the wealth is still anathema to many CEOs. I had a conversation with the leader of a hotel chain, and I suggested to him that he should raise all wages to a minimum of $16 an hour. He told me he could do so only if his competitors did, or else he'd be at an economic disadvantage.

"Really?" I said. "Are you sure of that?" I told him he was looking only at labor costs, not quality of service, productivity, morale, or retention.

That's our challenge. CEOs know that they can pay their lowest-wage employees seven, eight, or ten dollars an hour, because so many people are willing to work for that rate. These executives have no incentive to raise wages because, in their eyes, that will reduce short-term profits, which is often tied to their own compensation. This is myopic in every way possible. As Aetna discovered, paying your low-wage employees more money will help your organization in the long run, and it will also help the national economy, as more people will have the resources to buy the things businesses are trying to sell.

Whether the government should or shouldn't mandate a higher minimum wage is secondary. Companies should do it on their own.

Back at Aetna, we saw more opportunities for how we could make a difference in the lives of our employees, and we asked them to join us in a social compact. It essentially says: If you take care of yourself (in wellness and disease management programs), we will take care of you and your family.

We knew, for example, that many of our employees not only have college degrees but also student loans, so maybe we could help out. It's a staggering national problem—student debt stands at more than $1.3 trillion, affecting about 44 million borrowers. Nearly 70 percent of college graduates in the class of 2016 borrowed for their education, and they have an average of $37,000 of student debt. A 2016 EDAssist Student Loan Debt Survey highlighted how this was harming our economy: 50 percent of respondents said their college debt prevented them from buying a home, while 56 percent said they could not purchase a car. More troubling was that 77 percent of respondents said their personal relationships had been affected, and 49 percent said they would delay marriage or engagement.

In a perfect world, or at least a better world, our government would recognize the seriousness of this problem and take steps to remedy it. But that's not our world, and that's why companies have to fill the leadership void.

Aetna already had an employee tuition assistance program, which reimburses for 80 percent of approved expenses for attaining a college degree or for job-related college courses, but we raised the amount to $5,000 a year from $3,000. Then, in 2017, we began matching employees' student loan payments of up to $2,000 annually, with a lifetime maximum of $10,000.

We know that financial security has a direct impact on one's mental and emotional health, so we believe these moves will ease some financial burdens as well as contribute to our employees' well-being.

In that same spirit, we recognize that good health not only occurs during your waking hours but is very much dependent on your sleep. When my own body was shot through with pharmaceuticals, I rarely slept through the night, which only deepened my malaise. To encourage our employees to get sufficient rest, we decided to pay those who were willing to sleep at least seven hours a night, which we tracked using wearable devices. We paid $300 for seven hours sleep for twenty consecutive nights. Most people thought our rationale was that a well-rested employee is more productive. That's true, but it vastly understates the role that sleep plays in overall wellness. The body's inability to sleep creates a cycle that drives the body to a place in which it can no longer cope. Sleep deprivation is literally a killer. When you lose too much sleep, your heart can't modulate itself and you risk having a heart attack. Sleep disorders themselves can lead to tragedy. To address his sleep disorder, Michael Jackson was prescribed large doses of Propofol, an anesthetic, and Jackson died from cardiac arrest, with acute Propofol intoxication.

My friend Arianna Huffington has tapped into the importance of sleep in her bestselling books, but most Americans still have little appreciation for how it is connected to the opioid epidemic, PTSD, depression, and other ills. My belief is that sleep, just like meditation, just like yoga, is part of a wellness mosaic—affirmative acts that individuals can engage in to ensure a more vibrant physical, emotional, and spiritual self. I'm also convinced that for most people, once they've slept for seven hours a night for twenty or more days, they will continue doing so without any economic incentive. Their improved quality of life is more than enough incentive.

Given that many of these initiatives relate to my own experiences, I guess it's not surprising that I saw value in another unusual workplace gambit—pet therapy. I've loved dogs my whole life and know full well how they can connect with people. One of my favorite dogs was Dakota, our golden retriever who was with us in Boston when Eric was sick. Back in Avon, before my accident, I used to wake up at five-thirty in the morning and jog four miles, with Dakota running beside me stride for stride. One winter morning, I jumped off our front porch, fell on the ice, and slid on my back all the way down the driveway. Dakota watched my pratfall, jumped on the ice, and slid down right behind me.

My ski injury ended those morning jogs, and I'm telling you, Dakota knew I was hurt. I could see it in her face, in her body language. We could no longer do the things we did together, and she was devastated. She died about a year later, at age eleven.

I adopted other dogs, and when I became CEO, I would sometimes bring Lucky, a golden retriever, into the office. She came so often, she had her own badge with her name and photo—"Lucky Bertolini"—and she walked down the halls liked she owned the place. The cameras followed her, and wherever she went, people would pet her and enjoy her company. She was a company dog. One day when I was on the road, Lucky was at home, moping. She was stuck. She was also bothering Mari, so Mari called the office, and someone picked up Lucky and took her to the office. She went to work! She hung out there for the day, wandered in and out of my office, and was then taken home. I'm surprised she didn't ask for a raise.

It dawned on our head of benefits that other employees would enjoy spending time with a dog during their breaks, and there are organizations that bring in animals for just that purpose. That was how our pet therapy program began. We offer the program in our buildings all over the country, and the dogs come in on a regular basis—I was in our Chicago office, and we had four dogs there, with employees lined up down the hall to spend time with them. At some work sites, our employees wanted to bring in more types of animals, a true menagerie, so we now have kittens, rabbits, and guinea pigs as well. They also wanted mini ponies. I said no. I love mini ponies, but I have to draw the line somewhere.

DOMINIC BARTON, McKinsey's global managing partner, once asked me how I developed this progressive workplace strategy, from yoga to higher wages to cockapoos in conference rooms. My answer was, I didn't have a strategy. I never sat down with a piece of paper and sketched out a five-step employee plan that would increase engagement, boost morale, and augment disposable income. For starters, I don't do anything by myself. I need a great team around me. But also, each move happened organically. I didn't know that one initiative would lead to the next, but that's what happens when you change the culture of an organization. Our effort sent the message to our employees that they have permission to think differently about the workplace, and each program that we introduced has now been expanded or refined based on suggestions from our employees.

This approach is an extension of the trust model. Give your employees permission to take risks. Embrace change. Take care of one another. And all of that will lead to greater teamwork, higher morale, and more innovation.

Call it radical capitalism. As corporate leaders, we have the obligation to try to make life better for employees both at home and at work, and they will reciprocate not only by making your company better but also by improving their communities, the economy, and just maybe capitalism itself.

As Doc Holliday said, "It's all just life."

10

ECONOMIC FLYWHEEL

AFTER I WAS NAMED CEO, AETNA'S LARGEST SHAREHOLDER said he wanted me to increase the dividend. I said no. I thought that reinvesting our money back into the company would better serve Aetna's long-term interests. The shareholder wasn't pleased, and I told him if he didn't like that approach, he could get out of our stock. Which he did.

It's a perennial tension, especially for public companies: Do you maximize short-term gains at the expense of long-term profits? Or do you make short-term sacrifices for the possibility of increased profits down the road? The key word is *possibility*, because uncertainty is embedded in any long-term investment, whereas companies can take all kinds of steps to generate quick profits. What's more, virtually all incentives in corporate America are aligned to focus on immediate gratification. Wall Street punishes quarterly setbacks. Social media and cable TV pundits stir up impatient shareholders. A company's stock price heavily influences the compensation of its top leaders, some of whom are already in the stretch run of their careers. Thus, the mind-set: keep the share price high, collect the bonus, retire a hero, and leave the problems for the next generation of leaders.

I was once in a meeting in which senior executives were discussing the life insurance sales of a prior employer. The policies were sold by third-party agents who received commissions, so the company incurred immediate costs upon their sale but then received revenues through premiums for decades to come. The product led to short-term losses and long-term gains. Well, our own company sold the same product, and a couple of the executives in the meeting suggested that we reduce sales for the next couple of years so we could lower our costs and give our earnings an immediate lift.

"Wait a second," I said. "What about ten years from now?"

"Don't worry," one of them said. "We won't be here by then."

In this case, we did the right thing—we continued selling our life insurance product. If we had halted sales for even one year, our distributors would be so angry with us they might have stopped selling our product beyond that one year. Though we discussed impairing the business for immediate gains, the longer-term view prevailed.

Achieving long-term success should be every corporate leader's goal, and I've been influenced on this topic by Clayton Christensen, the Harvard business professor who is best known for his theory on disruptive innovation. Clay is that rare academic whose ideas on management, organizational behavior, and entrepreneurship have made a real impact in the business world. I heard him speak in Boston to a group of CEOs, and I was so impressed, I called him and asked if I could come by his office. He has studied virtually every major industry and has written eloquently not only about business but also about his experiences as a missionary in Korea and about how to live a fulfilling life. He evokes Jimmy Stewart—the lanky, droll, self-deprecating oracle who gently dispenses wisdom on the most important matters facing humanity.

I arrived at Clay's office, and it seemed typical of any office of an academic genius. It was cluttered, with papers strewn everywhere. Clay was fumbling around and seemed anxious.

"What's wrong?" I asked him.

"My office is such a mess," he said.

"You're a professor!" I said. "It's supposed to be a mess."

"Yeah, but I'm nervous."

"Why?"

"Because I've never had a CEO in my office."

Our thirty-minute meeting lasted three hours, with Clay taking out his whiteboard to sketch out some of his ideas. I specifically wanted to talk about health care, but the conversation veered into broader topics of corporate governance and leadership. He said that for the most part, shareholders are too focused on earnings per share. Shareholders themselves, he noted, do not benefit directly from increases in EPS. They benefit when they buy low and sell high. And what drives a stock price? It's Wall Street's belief in whether you have a sustainable product that your customers will consistently buy. That faith in the future is reflected in the P/E ratio. If investors believe your business fundamentals are sustainable over time, that will increase your P/E ratio, and that's how you need to think about your company. Don't manage the earnings. Anyone who does that is making a big mistake. Manage the business fundamentals—invest in a sustainable model— and the earnings will come.

Amazon is the classic example of a company that made long-term investments at the expense of immediate gains. Founded in 1994, Amazon by 2009 had lost more money than it had earned. But it continued investing in its business, particularly its immensely profitable cloud computing unit. In the P/E scenario, the "E" finally came—and so did the

"P/E." From March 2008 to March 2018, Amazon's stock price increased by 2,279 percent, and its market capitalization topped $1 trillion in 2018. And Amazon has never paid a dividend.

Whether you're Amazon or any other company, investing for the long term only works if you understand what customers want, and here again, Clay had a useful story, about McDonald's and its milk shakes.

When McDonald's was trying to increase its milk shake sales, it conducted focus groups and asked its customers for characteristics of the ideal milk shake (by flavor, thickness, etc.). Using that feedback, McDonald's tried to improve the taste, but it didn't matter. Sales remained flat. So the company hired Clay to see if he could figure out what was going on. Clay sent a colleague to one of the restaurants for a full day, and he documented who bought the milk shakes, at what time, whether the customers were by themselves or with others, and whether they drank the product at the restaurant or took it with them. Clay's colleague noticed that about 50 percent of the milk shakes were bought before 10 a.m., and the customers took the drink with them. The researcher returned the following day, stood outside the restaurant, and asked the milk shake buyers why they had "hired" that milk shake and for what job—an important construct in Clay's model. The customers offered a range of explanations. They said they didn't have time for breakfast and needed something that was quick; that they had a long, boring commute and needed something to keep that extra hand busy; that they knew they'd be hungry by 10 a.m. and wanted something to stave off that hunger until lunch. One thing was clear: nobody was hiring the milk shake for its taste.

According to Clay, we need to understand what consumers

are hiring their products to do. In this case, they were hiring the milk shake to occupy them in the car and to fill them up on their way to work. These customers were less willing to hire other foods, such as bagels or doughnuts, because those are messy; or a banana, because that's not filling enough; or even a Snickers bar, because that's untidy and makes you feel guilty. Once McDonald's understood the job that the milk shake was hired to do, it could ensure that the job was met. McDonald's developed a purchase card so that customers could go right to the milk shake machine and get their drink. McDonald's altered the milk shake cup so it more easily fit in cupholders, and it made the shakes thicker, with the option of fruit chunks, so it took more time to suck through the straw. According to Clay, milk shake sales increased by 30 percent.

Now, health insurance is a different animal. Many of our customers have our policies because their employer assigns Aetna to them. In addition, many of our products are close in price and features to those of our competitors. We needed to differentiate ourselves and connect with customers (employers or individuals), so they wanted to hire our products. We did this, in small part, by offering more information on the front end, particularly through digital platforms. But what we're really trying to do is promote our members' health and well-being. That's the most humane approach, because health is better than sickness. It's also the best business approach, because it increases the loyalty of our members and because our expenses decline if our members stay healthy (a single trip to an emergency room costs on average $1,800).

But there's the rub. We can only help our members stay healthy if we are willing to make significant investments in them—which means incurring short-term costs for unknown benefits in the future. It's really no different from our investments in our employees, but regarding our members, we already had a case study to prove that investing in them worked.

Medicare Advantage was passed in 2003, and it gave senior citizens and disabled Americans access to new and different private health plan options. The Centers for Medicare and Medicaid Services wanted private insurers to recruit and take on the less healthy—and more expensive—members of Medicare.

We agreed, as long as CMS paid us for our risk.

We developed a risk adjustment model, which looked at the medical profile of Medicare members and their use of services, and we priced our Medicare Advantage product accordingly. We rolled out the program in 2006, and it hinged on providing superior up-front care to reduce the higher average medical costs of this cohort.

When we began, CMS would pay us $900 a month for a 75-year-old person with three chronic comorbidities. CMS subsequently introduced a five-star rating system, in which insurers were evaluated on their care (for example, do plans ensure that diabetic patients regularly get a hemoglobin A1c test, which measures glucose levels for the past three months). Insurers that notch at least four stars receive a 5 percent bonus on monthly premiums.

The incentives gradually aligned. If we truly invested in the health of these individuals—if we intervened so that they experienced fewer health emergencies and fewer trips to the hospital—everyone would win: the members would be in better health, the government would save money, and we'd turn a profit.

The question was whether we could intervene to make a big enough impact on such a high-risk population.

If you ask a large group of senior citizens, "How many

prescriptions are you on?" they'd really struggle to answer that. They'd say, "I've got this green pill, I've got this pink pill, I've got this red pill." So-called polypharmacy is rampant. The sickest people on Medicare have on average twenty-four different prescriptions as well as a jumble of providers scattered at different offices and clinics.

For the Medicare Advantage program, we had an Aetna nurse visit the home or the apartment of our member, sit down with that individual, and ask some questions. "What drugs are you on?" "How many doctors do you see?" "What foods are you eating?" "Are you warm enough at night?" We tried to reduce the number of drugs and doctors to a manageable size. We looked at charts, worked with nutritionists, consulted with family members, and ensured that follow-up appointments were kept. It was important just to be there, not only to see that basic needs were cared for but also to maintain that human connection.

This type of steady engagement is expensive, especially when the numbers reach tens of thousands, hundreds of thousands, and now—for Aetna—more than 2.2 million Medicare Advantage members. But that type of engagement is precisely what works to minimize hospitalizations and other expensive therapies or procedures, and that's how we generate margins to reinvest in the business. When we reduce the health care costs of a Medicare Advantage member by 50 basis points, that individual generates more margin than a healthy twenty-four-year-old commercial member who rarely uses health care.

When we began the Medicare Advantage program, our critics said it could not be run profitably because of the health needs of this population. They're too old! They're too sick! Well, Medicare Advantage is now Aetna's fastest-growing business, and it's also an example of a successful public-private partnership. We've made engagement central to our entire mission, investing in creative ways to reach our members wherever they live. For example, we have a program with Meals on Wheels, which has 2 million volunteers who deliver meals to individuals four or five times a week. The volunteers know these people, and, they will tell you, it's not about the meals. It's about the friendship, it's about the personal interaction. We helped the organization build an app and asked the volunteers, with permission from the recipients, to notify us if there was any change in that person's mental capacity, mobility, or access to food, water, or heat. Let us know if that person needs a Lyft ride to the senior center or a ramp to be built for a wheelchair. Those investments will pay off, we said, in every way possible.

As for the business model, note that my focus is on margins, or revenues minus costs, *not* on earnings. Earnings are what we report each quarter. That's the output. That's what Wall Street cares about. But the goal is to generate margins, which gives us the capital to do any or all of four different things: pay dividends, build capabilities internally, acquire capabilities from others, or buy back shares. If we deploy that capital wisely to our other businesses, that will continue to create a sustainable business proposition for our customers. Investors will recognize that proposition, and our P/E will move faster than our earnings.

This approach offers lessons for every company in every business.

The easiest way to manage earnings is to use the levers that you control and then throttle them quickly. In any given year, I can easily lower my expenses to shore up my income statement. But driving top-line revenue growth is far more difficult. Your customers are fickle. Your competitors are aggressive. Your investors are impatient. And your own employees may not rally behind your plan. It takes courage and conviction to forgo the comfortable path of the status quo and make bold investments for the future, particularly unconventional investments centered on your own employees or customers. You have to embrace the risk. But once you've identified your customers' unmet needs, they will "hire" you and your product, and they will continue to reward you.

That's what happened to us. From 2010 to 2017, Aetna's operating (or adjusted) earnings per share increased by 124 percent, but our share price increased by 504 percent. (The S&P 500 increased by 125 percent.) Why the disparity between our operating earnings and our share price? In part because investors believed that our business fundamentals were sustainable over time. We invested in our employees and our members, and their value continued to grow. Our revenues increased, which generated margins, and we further reinvested that money into the business, and that created an economic flywheel in which the company kept growing, kept reinvesting, kept prospering. That's what great companies do. They produce margins that are reinvested in the company to enhance the value proposition for their members. Meanwhile, shareholders make money by buying low and selling high.

I don't know what became of our shareholder who demanded that I raise the dividend when I became CEO, but the dividend was 40 cents a share in 2010, and by 2017, it was $2 a share. Even more important, the stock price rose from $39 per share to $162 per share. Things worked out, over time.

11

MASTERS OF THE UNIVERSE, REINVENTED

IN 2018, THE *NEW YORK TIMES* WEBSITE TOUTED THE RE-
view of two books "on how companies and governments are
poisoning citizens and fraying the fabric of society." *Poisoning*? Quite an allegation. But it captured the zeitgeist. Americans have always had a deep distrust of government, which
dates back to our revolutionary roots. But I've also watched
with concern the growing disdain for companies and their
leaders—the belief that they are not only self-absorbed or
greedy but that they impede social and economic progress as
well.

It wasn't like that when I was young. Back then, corporate leaders were revered figures who bestrode the country on
missions to expand their own business empires while also en-
suring American supremacy. It was quite the gig. These men
provided the industrial might to conquer enemies in far-flung
wars. They led engineering and technological breakthroughs
that transformed all aspects of daily life. They poured money
into civic causes to strengthen our communities, and they
financed entrepreneurs who would become our next wave of
admired titans. They lived in mansions, drove big cars, and
toured the world, and when they got the CEO's brass ring,
they wore it with entitled splendor.

That idealized view could not survive decades of corporate upheaval, punctuated by scandals and personal failings.

Our top executives have experienced quite the fall. Presidential candidates routinely vilify those on Wall Street (until they need appointments to their new administration). Condemnation of insurers is one of the few things that unite the far left and the far right, and CEOs are now seen more often as the source of our ills instead of the remedy. This partly reflects the changing media landscape, which has diminished our trust in all business leaders—Alfred Sloan never had to respond to a tweet storm.

It's certainly true that corporate leaders make mistakes, and I won't make excuses for mine or anyone else's. But in marginalizing our influence, I believe something has been lost. Our experience. Our knowledge. Our voice. In my view, these are all needed. Our problems are such that our governance models, in both the public and private sectors, are no longer adequate. Broadband has eliminated traditional boundaries between and among nations, and the rapid flow of capital, goods, and data has become so fluid that our institutions have become virtually paralyzed in the face of our most difficult challenges. We can barely address, let alone solve, such problems as income inequality, drug addiction, climate change, and declining life expectancy.

I don't pretend to have all the answers, but I believe that corporate leaders have to be part of the solution. That can be done only if the public actually has faith in us. With rare exception, executives will never be seen in the same envious light as they were two generations ago. But that doesn't mean we cede the stage to our critics. We need to fight to regain that respect and through our actions restore the credibility of our leaders. I told my board that that was one of my goals. I didn't know how I would do it or if I had any chance of success, but I thought at minimum I could engage our political leaders in Washington and try to help them fix things in which I had some expertise. I'm not talking about lobbying or campaign contributions. I was interested in real work.

I was in for a surprise.

Health care reform was an obvious opportunity. Ron Williams had spent many days in Washington trying to help the Obama administration with the Affordable Care Act, which passed in 2010, my first year as CEO. I supported the intent of the law, and Aetna initially participated in more markets than any other private insurer. In 2011, I flew to Washington to talk to lawmakers about the ACA and to discuss what had to be done to ensure its success. Every piece of major social legislation, including Medicare and Medicaid, has been tweaked every year to adjust to new market conditions. But after a couple of meetings with lawmakers, I discovered that they weren't interested in the ACA or any other part of health reform. They told me straight up: *That's done. Now you figure it out.*

I wasn't sure what I was doing in Washington, but I found myself in a meeting with Senator Mark Warner, a Democrat from Virginia, who was part of a bipartisan group of senators (known as the "Gang of Six") trying to solve our country's federal debt. Warner explained their priorities to me and then absolutely took me to task: I had it easy running a company, he told me, whereas he was trying to do important work for the public good, and where the hell was my voice on the federal debt?

He had a point. I actually agreed that the federal government was incurring huge risks in accumulating so much debt, and I asked how I could help.

He told me to get some CEOs off their butts and get involved.

I told him I'd see what I could do.

I called John Engler, the former governor of Michigan who's a friend of mine and who was now the head of the Business Roundtable. We met for lunch, and I asked if his organization would release a letter, signed by a bunch of CEOs, in support of the Gang of Six. He agreed. I helped recruit the CEOs, and Engler released the letter. It didn't make a huge splash, but it showed that we made the effort. Warner called me back and thanked me, and he invited me to his house for a dinner meeting with about a dozen heavyweights to discuss the same issue. I attended and sat between Alice Rivlin and Alan Greenspan, with Paul Volcker across from me. I was the only businessperson there, and at one point, Warner asked me to address everyone.

I kept it simple. "We need to stand up and make clear the connection between our businesses and the federal debt, and if we don't step up and say what we need to do and what government needs to do, it will never happen. So, I think we need to get business rallied behind this issue."

It was hardly profound, but afterward I was approached by Maya MacGuineas, the president for the Committee for a Responsible Federal Budget. She said we needed to take this to a new level, and that was the birth of Fix the Debt, a nonpartisan organization with politicians, business leaders, and economists. We had some really smart people involved (David Cote, the chairman and CEO of Honeywell International, was its cochairman), and I thought we had a compelling argument: If the federal debt continued on its current trajectory, it would become a drag on the economy as a greater percentage of government spending would go to debt service, and if our near-historic low interest rates were to spike—say, to 7 percent—we'd have our next financial crisis. Complacency, which contributed to our last financial meltdown, should not be an option.

We held meetings, got some press attention, and met with both Republican and Democratic leaders, including Mitch McConnell and Harry Reid. Most everyone was sympathetic to the cause, but in Washington, money talks. We decided to invite corporate leaders to a $1-million-a-plate dinner, as a way to raise millions of dollars, to be used to rally support and to pressure lawmakers to take the necessary steps—some combination of tax increases and spending cuts—to bring down the debt.

Alas, Fix the Debt didn't fix anything. In July 2011, and facing a debt ceiling crisis, the Gang of Six introduced a bill that proposed to reduce the debt by $3.7 trillion over the next decade. It drew some positive media reviews and some endorsements from lawmakers in both the House and the Senate, but it didn't draw enough support. Congress, in a deal signed with President Obama, raised the debt ceiling to avert shutting down the government. No leadership from the White House. No leadership from Congress. No leadership from either political party. When we began our effort, the federal debt was $13 trillion. It's now more than $20 trillion. In light of the $1.5 trillion tax cut (give or take a few billion) that Congress passed into law in 2017, our debt will continue to soar.

In retrospect, I probably should have known better. Since I began my career, I've had under my desk blotter these lines from Machiavelli's *The Prince*:

> *It must be considered that there is nothing more difficult to carry out nor more doubtful of success nor more dangerous to handle than to initiate a new order of things; for the reformer*

has enemies in all those who profit by the old order, and only lukewarm defenders in all those who would profit by the new order; this lukewarmness arising partly from the incredulity of mankind who does not truly believe in anything new until they actually have experience of it.

Politics in America have their own eternal truths. One US senator told me my efforts were doomed: "Bertolini, you are the master of the universe. What you say at your company goes, but I have to get reelected."

And the millions of dollars that we raised for the cause? Most of it remains unspent, though to Maya's credit, she continues to speak out against fiscal irresponsibility.

It would be tempting to conclude from this experience that CEOs should just tend to their own gardens and let the politicians worry about our larger economic and social problems. But I draw the exact opposite lesson. I believe that in the absence of political leadership, business leaders must fill the void, and we must do it not as a matter of altruism or charity but of necessity. Other CEOs have come to that conclusion as well.

Larry Fink, as a cofounder of BlackRock, helped create America's largest asset management company (BlackRock is also Aetna's largest shareholder). In 2017, he wrote a letter to the country's CEOs, and it said in part:

We . . . see many governments failing to prepare for the future, on issues ranging from retirement and infrastructure to automation and worker training. As a result, society is increasingly turning to the private sector and asking that companies respond to broader societal challenges.

Those challenges are many, but I would put gun violence near the top. The bloodshed is too great to ignore.

In 2016, the year of the Pulse shooting, 38,551 people died in America by a firearm, according to the Centers for Disease Control and Prevention. (More than 60 percent of those were by suicide.) The latest data shows that we have had 317 mass shootings in 2018 as of November 11, 2018. The numbers have always been high, but we saw a turning point in the gun debate after the high school shooting in Parkland, Florida, in February 2018. Eighteen students were killed. In media interviews, protests, and rallies, the students who survived made their voices heard, and they were joined by many other young people. And companies listened.

Dick's Sporting Goods—one of the nation's largest gun retailers—announced that it would stop selling assault-style rifles and would ban the sale of all guns to anyone under twenty-one. Another major gun retailer, Walmart, had stopped selling assault rifles in 2015, and then in 2018 it stopped selling guns to anyone under twenty-one. Walmart even stopped selling items resembling assault-style weapons, including air guns and toys. Kroger said it would phase out gun sales at its Fred Meyer superstores.

Even companies that did not sell guns found ways to express their outrage. They "boycotted" the National Rifle Association, or at least ended their partnerships with it. Most of these companies were consumer enterprises, including Allied Van Lines, Avis, Chubb, Delta Air Lines, Enterprise, Hertz, MetLife, Symantec, and United Airlines.

Business leaders have found their voice against President Trump, expressing opposition to his immigration ban, which mainly affects majority Muslim countries. These leaders' views were driven not necessarily by alleged racism (as a candidate, President Trump vowed to ban Muslims) but by their reliance on immigrants with work visas. Ninety-seven companies, including many of the nation's largest—Amazon, Apple, Google, Facebook, Microsoft—filed a legal brief against the ban, saying it "inflicts significant harm on American business." The US Supreme Court ultimately upheld it.

President Trump's desire to deport "Dreamers," or the children of undocumented immigrants who are now living in the United States, has forged unlikely alliances. Apple CEO Tim Cook, one of the business world's most prominent progressives, and Charles Koch, a conservative libertarian who gives generously to Republicans, wrote an op-ed in the *Washington Post* calling on Congress to pass legislation to protect the Dreamers. "We are business leaders who sometimes differ on the issues of the day," they wrote. "Yet, on a question as straightforward as this one, we are firmly aligned."

I've told members of the House and the Senate essentially the same thing: "It seems on guns and immigration," I said, "our children have become pawns in a political debate. How can it come to this?"

But it has. Just as Congress has failed to address the federal debt, it has refused to pass any meaningful legislation on either guns or immigration, and to the shame of our lawmakers, the Dreamers remain in limbo.

For those in the business community, the test of leadership is whether we are willing to take stands on issues that risk alienating our customers or our employees to advance more important values or beliefs. We have seen that with guns, and I've been involved in the fray.

I've long believed that we need stricter gun laws, but I'm not your typical gun control advocate. I'm a gun owner—I have a 1911 Kimber pistol and a Smith & Wesson 642 hammerless revolver. I have permits to carry them, which I do when I believe I will be in a dangerous environment. I used to own a long rifle and a shotgun, but I got rid of them after my accident because I could no longer use them safely. I grew up in a hunting family and was always surrounded by guns. During the riots in Detroit in 1968, my dad kept a loaded shotgun at the front door. He also kept them under the bed. But he was never reckless. He taught me how to use guns properly and how to be careful with them, which I always have.

So, I'm hardly an enemy of the Second Amendment, but in recent years the school shootings have pushed me to the edge. After the Sandy Hook killings in Newtown, Connecticut, in 2013, I was a strong advocate of the state's sweeping gun control laws, which banned the sale of gun magazines and implemented background checks. In 2018, following the shooting in Parkland, Aetna donated $200,000 to the gun reform rally March for Our Lives, which took place in Washington and in cities all across America.

Critics of the rally flooded my email box. Some people complained that I was trying to repeal the Second Amendment. I also received thousands of form emails, apparently coordinated by the NRA, asking how Aetna could support a gun safety march while the Aetna Foundation provided matching grants to employees who donated to Planned Parenthood. These individuals saw moral equivalence between the carnage of gun-related homicides and a legal medical procedure.

I even received a call from the head of a small manufacturer in Michigan who was using Aetna for his employees' insurance. He told me he was canceling the contract.

"Great," I told him. "Have at it. Go ahead."

I believe that whatever risk we assume in losing a customer is offset by creating a company that stands for certain values, which in turn will attract and retain smart, engaged workers who believe in our mission. Our team and our mission are worth far more than any one customer or even group of customers.

I knew from the Fix the Debt debacle how difficult it is to change laws or even make a difference in the political world. That should not be the primary motive in taking a more aggressive or more public stance on issues. What should drive us is creating a corporate culture that prepares the next generation of great leaders. We have to recognize that millennials have different priorities than I had when I was their age. Their priorities are, in order, people, planet, and profits. Millennials have been influenced by what they have seen and experienced—a world with vast income inequality, in which the wealthiest distance themselves behind golden barricades; a planet endangered by climate change, with rising sea levels, melting snowcaps, and raging forest fires, and a country in which only 30 percent of adults believe their children will do better than they did.

For millennials, the capitalist model cannot simply be about maximizing earnings and increasing shareholder value, which means leaders can no longer ignore the first two P's—people and planet. We must speak out on these issues and have a point of view that is respectful, fair, and humanistic. This, of course, is not a CEO's traditional role, but I realized it was my role when I was doing town hall meetings. People were asking me questions that did not deal directly with our business operations but centered on social and cultural issues. I would get the same questions on my blog. What was my view? What was our company's view? I either told them, or I said we didn't have a view yet but would get back in touch. Either way, I didn't shy away from sensitive topics.

I write opinion pieces, I pen blogs, I give speeches, I give interviews, I tweet, I retweet, I ruffle feathers. I was one of about twenty-five CEOs who called for an end to travel and entry restrictions for people who are living with HIV. Above all, I try to have a running conversation with our employees. Our workers can go to our internal website and read the company's position on any number of issues or topics. They can type in where they live and see who represents them in Congress, with those individuals' emails and office phone numbers displayed. Our objective is not to tell employees what to think but to tell them what the company thinks—and what I think—because that's what they expect from us.

Do we risk losing employees who don't share our views? Yes, but the employees who don't share our views on some of these issues, such as gun safety, immigration, and same-sex marriage, would probably be happier at another organization.

Our goal is to reinforce the values of the company, prepare it for the next generation of leaders, and nurture those who will follow us.

We will never again have the heroic CEOs of my youth, but we can still have deeply admired business leaders who reflect the best in America, and those leaders will be far more representative of our changing country: more women, more people of color, and more strivers from more diverse backgrounds. Those who succeed will be authentic, approachable, and willing to speak out on the most important issues of the day. They will be their own masters of the universe, reinvented.

12

REIMAGINING THE FUTURE

IN FEBRUARY 2014, CVS ANNOUNCED THAT IT WOULD stop selling cigarettes from its 7,700 retail pharmacies, making it the first major pharmacy chain to implement such a ban. The move would cost CVS $2 billion a year in revenue. CVS and Aetna already had a partnership, with CVS providing pharmacy benefits and management services to our customers. On the day that CVS announced its cigarette ban, I called the company's CEO, Larry Merlo.

I was the first to congratulate him.

"Kudos to you, man," I said. "That is courageous. I love having a partner like you."

I told him that we should get together and talk about what's next strategically for our companies and our industry. It took a while, but the following year, Larry and I met for dinner at Peppercorn's in Hartford.

"Mark," he said, "I have to tell you something. Every time I do something like cigarettes and I improve the health of the population, I take a revenue hit, and you win."

"Thank you, Larry," I said. "That's true. That's because you have the wrong revenue model. You make money on a fee-for-service basis. I make money by keeping people healthy. You need a different revenue model, and if you continue doing the things that you're doing, our revenue model is the right one."

I suggested the two companies should find other ways to work together. Larry was interested, and we discussed different types of alliances and partnerships, including combining the two companies. But I told him we couldn't do anything right now because Aetna was in the midst of another transaction. When that was complete, I said, we'd continue the conversation.

We were closing in on our acquisition of Humana. I told my team that when that deal was finalized, we'd buy CVS and change the health care industry.

I LIKE TO fix things that are broken, and that skill has defined my entire career (the media call me "Mr. Fix-it"). When my kids ask me what I want for my birthday, I always tell them I want to drive a Zamboni machine, which is used to smooth the ice after each period in a hockey game. The Zamboni driver always follows the same pattern, and I'm obsessed with the notion that I can find a better pattern. I want to fix things even when they're not broken! (And my kids, wisely, buy me something more practical.)

No one disputes that our health care system is broken, but fixing it will require some unconventional thinking. That a health insurer would buy a pharmacy chain is certainly unconventional—such a merger, as far as I knew, had never been contemplated—but it fit precisely with what I was envisioning for the future of health care.

Aetna's mission is to "build a healthier world," and it starts at home. I view our health care system through a unique prism. I've been a worker, a manager, or an executive in the industry for more than four decades. I saw it up close, in its glory and its failings, with Eric. And I continue to experience it firsthand, intensely, gratefully, and inadequately, with my own injuries.

Consider how our health system works. You buy insurance and you get a card. You pull out that card when you get sick or sustain an injury, and you go to a clinic or a hospital, and then the system throws you back into your life. That's how we take care of people—no sustained engagement in you as an individual, no effort to understand what your needs might be. Our system is mainly reactive: it responds to illness or injury but is otherwise detached from the daily lives of most Americans. That approach may have been adequate at one time, but our country's social and economic ruptures have exposed its unsuitability to our current needs.

In 2015, the researchers Anne Case and Angus Deaton published a paper that documented the dramatic rise in deaths among middle-aged white Americans, driven not by conventional disease but by suicide, drugs, alcohol, and loneliness. The report stunned many commentators, as these "deaths of despair," as they were called, seemed beyond the reach of our $3.3 trillion medical-industrial complex.

Opioid abuse rightfully drew much of the attention. Eighty percent of all opioids produced in the world are consumed by Americans, or enough to keep every American stoned for six weeks. The scourge is only getting worse. According to the National Center for Health Statistics, opioids were blamed for 34,572 deaths in 2016, a 52 percent increase from 2015. Drug fatalities overall in 2016 reached a staggering 72,000, and even that number does not reflect the millions of Americans who have been compromised, incapacitated, or removed from the workforce because of drugs. According to a study by the American Action Forum, nearly 1 million people were not working in 2015 due to opioid addiction. It's no wonder that American productivity has stagnated rapidly: according to the Bureau of Labor Statistics, between 2013 and 2017, manufacturing productivity increased at an average annual rate of 0.44 percent, compared to an average annual rate of 2.7 percent between 1987 and 2017.

I speak from personal experience when I say that we should not forget what opioids are designed to do: kill pain. The countless headlines about the epidemic are a screaming reminder that a large swath of America is in one type of pain or another, but our health care system and our government have few answers on how to respond.

The cumulative toll, from opioids and other threats, is grim.

In 2015 the life expectancy of an American declined for the first time since 1993, when the HIV/AIDS epidemic was still running high. Life expectancy dropped again in 2016. According to the National Center for Health Statistics, death rates are ballooning across virtually all major diseases and rising or staying the same for every demographic. This defies everything we thought was true about our health care system, in which extraordinary advances in medical technology, diagnostics, and individual therapies were lifting us to ever-higher plateaus of wellness. Instead, we are dying younger, and we are killing ourselves more often. In 2018, the CDC reported that suicide rates rose steadily in nearly every state from 1999 to 2016; the CDC attributed this increase to social isolation, lack of mental health treatment, drug and alcohol abuse, and gun ownership.

America loves to compare itself to other countries, as a sign of our progress and preeminence. But when it comes to heath, we are faring worse compared to other developed countries. According to the Commonwealth Fund, a foundation that supports research on health care, America in 2016 spent a far greater share of its GDP on health care (17.1 percent) than any other wealthy country in the world (the next highest was France, at 11.6 percent), but among the thirty-five nations in the Organisation for Economic Co-operation and Development, the United States had the highest obesity rates, led in drug-related deaths, and was thirty-third in the prevalence of diabetes. We were twenty-sixth in life expectancy, right above the Czech Republic but below Slovenia.

"This Century Is Broken," declared a 2017 headline in the *New York Times*, referring to our country's declining health, stagnant wages, and diminished social mobility. J. D. Vance's bestselling memoir, *Hillbilly Elegy,* became the explanatory text for Donald Trump's popularity among white working-class voters. I read it with personal interest. The actual "Hillbilly Highway" is US Route 23, named for those in Appalachia who migrated north; the highway runs through Kentucky and Ohio (where J. D. Vance is from), cuts right past metropolitan Detroit, and ends in northern Michigan. I grew up with plenty of transplanted "hillbillies." They had uprooted in search of a better life. They were willing to move, to strive, to take risks, which is all about seeking a better future. Vance, to my mind, profiled a group of people who were stuck in their community, amid dying industries and vanishing expectations—it is an elegy to the loss of hope, and it captured the emerging trend of immobility: Fewer people moved in 2017 than in any year in at least a half a century, according to ProPublica.

What does that have to do with health care? Everything.

If you're in pain; if you're not clearheaded; if you're addicted to drugs; if you're sluggish or depressed or lonely, you don't care about anything else. You won't have a steady job. You won't have an intact family. You won't be economically, socially, or physically mobile, and the American Dream will be something that you read about in a middle school history book.

That's why I believe if we're going to solve the big economic and social problems in our country, we have to start with health care. Toward that end, we need to rethink what our health care system should do and even redefine what health is.

I'm partial to the World Health Organization's definition of health, from 1948, as "a state of complete physical, mental, and social well-being and *not merely the absence of disease*" (my emphasis). That definition grasps the deeper and more holistic nature of health, yet very few people describe it in that fashion. Maybe the WHO's language does not speak directly enough to outcomes. We need something that is more affirmative and reflects the broader good of wellness, so I like to say that "a healthy person is productive; a productive person is socially, spiritually, and economically viable, and a viable person is happy."

How we get there begins by changing our understanding of health care from something that is *provided* by your employer or the government to a *journey* that you are in charge of. Consider what you do when you buy a car. You don't go to GM's headquarters and order one off the lot, and you don't go to GMAC or to some other lender. You go to a dealership, and you tell the dealer everything you want that car to be: the size, the color, the interior, the sound system, the trunk space, the seat covers, all the bells and whistles. You get the car that meets your needs, and then you develop a plan for how to pay for it.

Our health care system does the exact opposite. In most cases, we tell you about your health plan, and then you figure out whether it meets your needs. We need to flip that. What if we had a system in which your health insurer asked first about your health status and your goals in life? Those goals may be to watch your grandchild graduate from college or to climb Mount Kilimanjaro or to see your fiftieth wedding anniversary. We could then say, based on your current health and your long-term goals, let's design a set of benefits and a way to pay for them that would take care of you for life. That would be a much better experience than for you to buy a health insurance policy and wait until your knee is broken or your lungs don't work.

Next, let's recognize the importance of what most influences health, or the social determinants—from unclean water to unsafe streets, from the prevalence of drugs to the absence of nutritious food. We know from our own research that 10 percent of your life expectancy is associated with clinical care, 20 percent is related to where you live, 40 percent is influenced by your lifestyle, and 30 percent is related to your genetics. That means that 90 percent of the factors affecting premature death occur outside the doctor's office, hospital, or pharmacy, where we spend most of our health care dollars. What we don't invest in are social determinants, a failure that only commands our attention during a crisis—such as the unsafe drinking water in Flint, Michigan, which starting in 2014 exposed more than 100,00 residents to high levels of lead and where residents today still refuse to drink the cloudy tap water.

We see the practical effects of this failure in other ways. A 2014 study by the Robert Wood Foundation found that babies born in Montgomery County, Maryland, and neighboring counties in Virginia (Arlington and Fairfax) have a life expectancy six to seven years longer than those of babies born in Washington, D.C., just one zip code away. Washington, of course, is a much poorer community. Those kinds of jarring socioeconomic disparities between adjacent communities can be found in Baltimore, the Bronx, Bridgeport, my hometown of Detroit, and in cities and suburbs across America. In 2018, the Aetna Foundation worked with *U.S. News & World Report* to assess 3,000 communities in America and to rank the 500 healthiest. My home community in Michigan, Wayne County, didn't even make the list of 500, while the adjacent counties of Oakland and Washtenaw were in the top 300.

It's why I believe that as far as morbidity and mortality rates go, your zip code matters more than your genetic code. Or as David Nash, the dean of the Jefferson College of Population Health, said, "Where you are on the map predicts your life span."

We should be investing in those parts of the map that need the most help, but our overall spending is too low to make a difference. In the United States, our expenditures on social determinants, as a percentage of GDP, are ranked twelfth out of the top thirteen OECD countries, according to 2013 data compiled by the Peterson-Kaiser Health System Tracker.* We underinvest in the very things that can have a big impact for the same reason that companies underinvest in their

---

* Peterson-Kaiser notes that "varying models" exist to measure social determinants, but they generally include "individual and community behaviors, economic circumstances, and environmental factors."

employees or customers—their costs are immediate, their benefits long term.

Focusing on social determinants lies at the core of prevention, whose benefits should be self-evident. Fifty percent of the American population has a chronic disease, and they drive 86 percent of all health care costs. For that cohort, health care is not episodic; it's continuous. The goal is to intervene early to deter bad outcomes down the road. Even delayed interventions can be valuable. At Aetna, we had a seventy-eight-year-old female client with asthma, and in one year she made 405 visits to the emergency room (yes, more than once a day). Those visits cost $2.7 million. We sent a nurse to see her, and it turns out that she kept her thermostat at 60 degrees, so she often wore sweaters. Her friends made her angora sweaters, which she liked very much, except that she was allergic to angora!

It's a perfect demonstration of how preventive measures—in this case, a simple home visit—can improve people's health while reducing overall costs. Once you visit the person and make a health assessment, you can invest to improve outcomes. But as a country, we don't get close enough to the community or the home to generate better results.

Personal engagement also needs to be a top priority: how do we motivate individuals to care about their well-being, and how do we make that engagement meaningful? This is the Holy Grail of health care. Progress will not happen at annual checkups (too infrequent, too perfunctory) or at the hospital (too expensive, too late). Progress also won't occur through some "wellness program." Many organizations have a wellness program, and frankly they don't do much. The real question is, what motivates someone to act differently than they ordinarily would? And whom can we count on to provide that motivation?

The answer, in my opinion, is to become more local. We need to meet people where they're at, in their homes and communities, and find out what matters to them. In putting the individual first, we need to integrate the power of community and technology to engage that person in ways the current system does not.

What does that mean in practice?

Let's take a fictional sixty-two-year-old woman named Mary who has type 2 diabetes and lives by herself. She sees her doctor only twice a year, and those visits last fifteen minutes. But her neighbor Stacy visits her every two weeks to ensure that she is taking her medicine, has enough food, and is testing her blood sugar. Stacy is hired by Mary's insurer and is qualified to conduct health assessments. As a neighbor, Stacy knows Mary and is trusted by her. Equipped with a smartphone, Stacy sends health data to Mary's insurer and doctor. She also scans the house for loose rugs, broken thermostats, and other problems that could lead to an emergency. She asks Mary how much she's been sleeping, does she have fruits and vegetables in the house, what are her biggest worries—inquiries that allow us to track how Mary's health plan is working.

One day Mary tells Stacy that since her foot started hurting, she hasn't been able to take her daily walk to the park, where she reads a book. So Stacy drives Mary to a local pharmacy, which has been equipped with an urgent care center. The doctor examines the foot and recognizes early-stage diabetic neuropathy. By more aggressively controlling her blood sugar, Mary can reverse the problem, sparing her from painful long-term complications, including a possible amputation, and saving the health care system hundreds of thousands of dollars.

Which is fine by Mary but is not likely to motivate her. The specter of some future health calamity rarely changes behavior. In Mary's case, she mentions the foot in the first place because she wants to walk to the park to read her book. In short: *It's not about the foot. It's about the walk.* That's what matters to her, that's what motivates her. You need to meet people where they're at. The engagement needs to be personal and focused on what matters to the patient. In the current system, the "walk" doesn't even make the agenda.

The federal government is gradually beginning to accept some of these principles. In 2018, Congress, with support of both Republicans and Democrats as well as the Trump administration, passed a law that provides additional social and medical services to Medicare beneficiaries who have multiple chronic illnesses. These services include home improvements such as wheelchair ramps and bathtub railings, transportation, home visits by nurses, and home delivery of meals. David Sayen, a longtime administrator for CMS, told the *New York Times* that this new federal policy will give health plans "a whole new tool box to address social determinants of health."

Patient engagement also involves how providers talk about disease and injury, which I first learned during Eric's illness but have discovered in my own struggles.

A couple of years ago, I slipped on the ground outside and fractured my disabled left arm. My doctor wanted to put me in an arm brace for twelve weeks, but I didn't like that option because I wouldn't be able to ride my bike and because I figured it would just be a matter of time before I broke it again. I had read about a bionic arm, used by military vets who had lost limbs, and that arm allowed them to play the piano, type, and play sports.

I told my doctor that I wanted to amputate my arm and get one that worked for me.

He refused. "You have a perfectly functioning biological arm," he told me.

"But you're not living with it. It hurts all the time, and I can't use it for all the things I want to use it for."

So, we had a discussion. It was not about how to fix a humeral fracture. It was about who I am as a person and what my arm, broken or not, was preventing me from doing: riding my bike. We ultimately found a compromise: instead of a bionic option, my doctor increased the reach in my arm that allowed me to more easily ride my bike. The arm had been an inch short, due to a shoulder fusion from a prior injury. The doctor gave me a bone graft and lengthened the arm by an inch. I got an upgrade.

It may be an extreme example—and clearly, not everyone has the resources to consider these options—but the point still holds: once we define disease or injury by what it prevents us from doing and how it affects the lives that we want to lead, our conversation with our providers will be more productive, and patient engagement will improve.

In stressing the importance of health care in the home and the community, some history is in order. In the 1850s, we had an agrarian society, in which we built our own goods, made our own food, and took care of each other. Our communities were not wealthy, but what you had you shared to make sure everyone survived, and the community itself was the center of almost all interaction. That self-contained, self-regulated world could not survive the coming industrial and technological revolutions, and our contributions to the economy, as opposed to our community, came to define success. Neighborhoods became atomized, with our physical ties—and responsibilities—to each other increasingly frayed. Community lost meaning. Talk about it today to millennials, and they'll assume you're talking about an online chat group.

I'm not advocating that we return to the 1850s, and I'm not saying we can magically re-create a world that no longer exists. But we can learn from our past, and one thing that we lost from that era was the notion of a community taking care of its own across childhood, adulthood, and old age. The home used to be the center of care, but that was no longer the case once individuals had to visit their doctors in clinics or hospitals.

Technology is changing this dynamic, as the gig economy can broaden our pool of health care providers while slowly restoring the home—not the clinic or the hospital—as the nexus of care.

Just look at TaskRabbit, which matches local labor with needed jobs. The same can work with health care. Providers with different skill levels would sign up and say, "I'm available from nine to noon, or four to eight, and here is what I'm qualified to do." They would be paid by the insurer, which would be far cheaper than a visit to the ER. We would also be strengthening bonds among the people in the community, those who hopefully know you the best and are more likely to truly care about your well-being.

We want to move the conversation about your health from the exam table to the kitchen table. When you visit your doctor, you might get ten or fifteen minutes, and if the doctor asks you how much you're eating, exercising, or drinking, you'll probably offer misleading statements on at least some of those questions—assuming, of course, you even have a doctor. Surveys indicate that between 20 and 25 percent of people don't even have one.

That's why I want to bring the conversation to the kitchen table, where you're with people who know you and where people find out what's really going on: who's got a new job, who's selling their car, who's getting married or divorced. That's where your conversation about health should be.

That was the idea behind our Meals on Wheels partnership, in which the volunteers will notify us of changes in health status. Those kinds of jobs require transferring data or other communications among payers or providers, and all of that is now possible with smartphones and other communication devices. Just as the Digital Age has changed the workplace, it is now allowing for new kinds of home engagement.

Aetna, for example, has a program with our congestive heart failure patients, who are our most expensive. When they leave the hospital, we give them a scale and install it with Bluetooth technology. We ask that they weigh themselves each day, and when their weight rises to "out of tolerance," we see it ourselves and call their doctor, who can then intervene so that care is provided *before* the next episode. We're currently working with Medtronic because pacemaker readings detect blood-flow resistance; once the technology is developed to monitor that resistance remotely, even earlier intervention is possible.

The FDA has already approved wearable sensors that can continuously monitor all vital signs: blood pressure, heart rate, body temperature, breathing rate, oxygen concentration in the blood, and blood sugar. "The cost to do this for weeks would be a tiny fraction of the cost for a day in the hospital," said Dr. Eric Topal, a cardiologist who is a professor of molecular medicine at the Scripps Research Institute. Writing in the *Wall Street Journal*, he noted that ultrasound probes can now connect to smartphones to provide images comparable to those on hospital machines. "It is possible to examine any body part (except the brain) simply by connecting the probe to the base of a smartphone and putting a little gel on the probe's tip. . . . One obvious practical effect of these developments will be to replace hospital stays with remote monitoring in the patient's home."

Our health care system also needs greater personalization of care, or the tailoring of treatment and therapies that patients actually want and need. Many of us already seek this personalization when we choose our provider.

When Eric was released from Boston Children's Hospital in 2003, he swore he would never return to the city. Too many bad memories, too much pain, too much death. Well, Eric not only returned to visit Boston—he lived there for many years, and it wasn't because of the Red Sox. He settled in Boston because of his close ties with one of his doctors, Susan Parsons, who reversed the graft-vs.-host disease that was threatening to destroy Eric's skin. Eric knows he is still at risk—he retains a slight rash on his shoulder as evidence of his graft-vs.-host condition—so he wanted the care of Dr. Parsons: she knows his history, she understands his emotional needs, and she is trusted by Eric to keep this disease at bay.

That is one type of personalization, but we need to broaden the concept to include what I call a "curated" approach to care. We typically associate "curation" with a museum. When you walk into an art museum, perhaps 5 percent of the collection is on display. The rest is in storage. The museum doesn't show you everything because it knows that you're not interested in everything. It has curated the art that it believes is most meaningful to you. This notion needs to be applied to health, but with a twist. The curation will be done by the consumer, who wants access to therapies or services that most closely meet his or her needs. Technology is once again driving the change. For example, I have a friend who runs his young diabetic child's glucose numbers across the top of his smartphone screen from a continuous glucose monitoring device—a breakthrough that is transforming how that disease is managed but is still not covered by every health plan.

We've barely scratched the surface of consumer analytics in health care, and that data will personalize—and revolutionize—the industry. As *Fortune* magazine noted, "The amount of data you slough off every day—in lab tests, medical images, genetic profiles, liquid biopsies, electrocardiograms, to name just a few—is overwhelming by itself. Throw in the stuff from medical claims, clinical trials, prescriptions, academic research, and more, and the yield is something on the order of 750 quadrillion bytes every day—or some 30 percent of the world's data production."

The challenge is how we distribute, connect, wear, and exploit that information for each person's health journey, but with the likes of Google, Apple, Amazon, and many other companies entering or expanding into this market, those challenges will be met. Patients are sick and tired of being sick and tired, but personalized data will empower them, in concert with their providers and their insurer, to build a health plan that works for them.

A consumer revolt is coming, and it's easy to foresee. In employer-based health plans, workers are now paying for 41 percent of their overall health care costs including premium and benefits. At some point, employees will demand a greater say in how their money is being spent, and they will want coverage that applies to their needs—the curated experience.

In describing what our health care system should be, note that I'm not talking about "single payer" or "private payer" or any other kind of payer. Note also that I'm not talking about how we provide coverage for the uninsured. Those issues relate to how we *finance* care, and that is undoubtedly important. But it is not most important. We can change the financing of health care all we want, but if the system is broken, we'll still be financing poor outcomes at ever-higher costs.

In sum, we need a system that promotes health and wellness, and that system should do the following:

- Enlist the resources of the community, including storefronts and pharmacies, as the first line of defense against disease or sickness.
- Deploy friends, neighbors, and relatives in persistent, caring engagement.
- Recognize that social determinants are driving huge disparities in health outcomes across the country and invest accordingly.
- Invest in the prevention of disease, not just the treatment of symptoms.
- When people need care, provide a personal solution aimed at improved quality of life.

I had been thinking about these ideas ever since Eric's illness and had consulted any number of experts, and at Aetna, we had begun implementing a more consumer-oriented journey for our members. (Our new motto was "You don't join us, we join you.") We were making progress, but we needed to make deeper inroads into our communities, which brings me back to CVS.

No matter how many individuals we could enlist to reach our members in their homes or apartments, we could never reach enough of them. We needed to find a different way to reach greater numbers of people. Our competitors were thinking along the same lines. UnitedHealth Group, in a pilot program, had partnered with retail pharmacies at Walgreens, Kroger, and Safeway to help patients with type 2 diabetes, assisting with medication, nutrition, and blood glucose monitoring, all of which these patients once received at clinics.

We needed retail outlets in towns across America that would serve as the front door to our health care system. We weren't going to build them, so we needed a partner.

ON JULY 3, 2015, Aetna announced that it would purchase Humana for $37 billion, combining the country's third- and fourth-largest insurers. Humana has a significant Medicare Advantage business, which would have complemented ours, and it has the same commitment to patient engagement that we have. Our market cap at the time was around $44 billion. Once the acquisition was completed and the two companies were integrated, we'd have a big enough balance sheet to buy CVS, which would have made us America's second-largest publicly traded company by revenue, behind Walmart.

But the Humana deal didn't happen. The Department of Justice filed suit to block it; the DOJ did the same to stop the merger of two other large health insurers, Anthem and Cigna. In our case, because we would now be the dominant player in Medicare Advantage, a central issue was whether Medicare

Advantage competed with traditional Medicare products. The DOJ claimed they did *not* compete against each other, which—if true—meant that our strong position in Medicare Advantage ran afoul of antitrust laws. But the whole point of Medicare Advantage is to attract Medicare recipients with a more competitive product. The judge thought otherwise and, in January 2017, ruled against us and blocked the merger. A separate judge also blocked the Anthem-Cigna merger.

The ruling was a setback, but it did not deter us from our goal of broadening our footprint and finding new and better ways to engage patients. In that regard, one of the first calls I received after this setback, in February 2017, was from Larry Merlo at CVS.

"Do you still want to talk?" he asked.

I did.

WE GOT TOGETHER, and in these kinds of discussions, the first question is, what's the strategy? Our early conversations envisioned any number of partnerships between CVS and Aetna, including contractual agreements, joint ventures, and a merger.

My team and I were also talking to two other companies about possible combinations, but CVS represented the greatest opportunity. The company now has 9,700 retail locations and 1,100 clinics, and nearly 80 percent of the US population lives within five miles of one of its stores. If our goal was to move health care into the community, CVS was the most direct path to get there.

In the spring and summer months, my team and Larry's team had numerous meetings and conversations about what the two companies could do together. It took time. We didn't understand their business, they didn't understand ours. But I told Larry the same thing that I told Apple when we were discussing a partnership with the Apple watch: every 50 basis points that we reduce health care costs is $480 million in underwriting margin; so, in CVS's case, if we could build a model that reduces those costs—in greater patient engagement, increased adherence to medication, preventive care, and early intervention—everyone would win.

Academics talk about "disruption" in the market, and an alliance between CVS and Aetna could certainly be disruptive. But it's worth remembering that companies don't disrupt anything. Customers do. Amazon created an online platform, but it was the customers who disrupted the market. They wanted products that were fast, reliable, and cheap, and Amazon recognized that need and filled it. (That Amazon earns most of its money from cloud computing gives it additional power to keep its retail prices low.)

Like every brick-and-mortar retailer, CVS must now compete against Amazon and other low-cost, high-quality online businesses, but as Larry and I talked about this challenge, we agreed that for our efforts to succeed, the outcome had little to do with Amazon and everything to do with whether we could satisfy the unmet needs of our customers. What exactly did they want?

The health care system was the problem: It's confusing. It's impersonal. It's the largest line item in most people's budgets. And the whole process is horrifying.

I would also add, it doesn't keep people healthy. Its focus is to fix unhealthy people.

Larry and I gathered our teams, and we began developing a model that would make health care more accessible, more convenient, more intelligible, and more affordable. It all centered on transforming the role of the stores in the community: They are currently pharmacies that are attached to crowded aisles of potato chips, batteries, deodorant, greeting cards, gift cards, playing cards, and a whole lot more. Let's turn them into community health centers instead.

When I initially broached this idea with the CVS team, someone asked me if I wanted to expand the CVS MinuteClinic.

I said no. We don't need three more plastic molded chairs and a countertop. We need something much more radical. We need to create a venue that people actually want to visit.

Ron Williams used to say, "No one goes into a store and buys an Aetna." Instead, an Aetna product is sold to people because it's something they need. Similarly, most people go into a CVS because they have to buy something that they need. The store serves a function, but it could aspire to something greater. Other retailers take that approach.

George Blankenship designed the stores for the Gap, Apple, Microsoft, and Tesla, all of which create a warm environment that relaxes customers and creates a positive, even exciting experience. Blankenship once told the *New York Times* that at Tesla showrooms, the goal was "to never sell a car from there." He wanted people to ask to buy a car. It's a similar concept with Apple. You enter the store and pay money to visit the Genius Bar, and then you spend more money on your way out. You're so engaged in what you're seeing, so mesmerized, you want to buy something from Apple. Apple doesn't need to sell you anything.

A CVS store will never sell an electric car or a smartphone, but it can still be a place where people want to visit and say, wow, this is cool. As we envisioned this future CVS store, it will continue to sell health and beauty products and have a robust pharmacy, but most of the other consumer items will be cleared out, and the space will be devoted to improving the health of the community.

When you walk in, a greeter will ask, "How can we help you today?"

If you say, "I want to start running again, but I need a brace for my knee," the greeter will say, "Great, let me take you over here to get you fitted for one." We'll have a durable medical equipment area, and we'll have a professional who can fit you with a knee brace. We'll have a partnership with a retailer like REI, and we'll have stairs that you can practice on before leaving.

CVS MinuteClinics already provide a wide range of health services, but the new stores will expand those and also offer procedures or exams that have long been done in hospitals. For example, when a woman receives a mammogram, her doctor sometimes orders a CT scan. But the patient may have to wait two weeks, as the CT scan operators are only available from eight to five. The CVS stores could have a twenty-four-hour CT scan available. Women could receive the scan sooner, and because it's close and accessible, women would be more likely to get it in the first place. The same is true for other kinds of X-rays, or with infusions, or even dialysis. Aetna has oceans of data about our members, and we're developing models that tell us where the greatest opportunities are for investing in their health, be it through digital communication, personal visits, or other outreach efforts. As we continue to expand these efforts, the CVS locations will become an accessible front door for the system at large.

The conversations between Larry's team and mine continued into the summer and the fall of 2017. Our focus remained on the strategy, and we agreed that the best way to achieve our goals—a shift to lower-cost sites of health care services, improved quality of care, and improved care management—was for CVS to acquire Aetna.

We next talked about whether the cultures of the two companies would support those efforts, and finally we talked about price.

On October 11, I received a formal offer from Larry for CVS to buy all the shares of Aetna.

News of our negotiations leaked to the press, but we continued on, with a small army of investment bankers and lawyers trying to iron out the many details. Merger agreements are always a bear, and we were nearly complete when my team came to me and said that CVS wanted the ability, starting in May 2019, to change our benefits package for our employees. That included everything from health care to tuition reimbursement to yoga. They asked me what I thought. I told them I didn't really care about the benefits for the executives—they would be fine—but I would not sign any agreement that changed the benefits for our frontline employees. That was a commitment that we had made, and we would not renege on that promise.

I was willing to walk away from a $69 billion deal on that principle. CVS retained the benefits.

On December 3, the announcement was issued that CVS would be acquiring Aetna for $207 a share in a deal that could "reshape the health industry," according to the *Times*.

That's certainly the goal.

Health care is neither the first nor the last industry to face upheaval, and we already know what happens to those industries, or companies, that fail to adapt. No single brand, even among the most powerful, is immune. For decades, Eastman Kodak dominated film and camera sales. Then, in the 1970s, it invented digital photography and the first handheld digital camera. But the camera was expensive and, more important, it posed a direct threat to Kodak's crown jewel, its emulsion-coated film. The near-term result was that Kodak mothballed its new invention while spending many years trying to protect its intellectual property. The long-term result was the hollowing out of a once-great company, as Kodak's film business was eclipsed by superior technology: almost unlimited images provided instantly on a platform that allowed an amateur to create beautiful photographs. Even though Kodak invented that technology, it still missed the opportunity because it could not envision the world beyond the image—black and white or in color—of its glorious past.

It's a lesson that repeats itself throughout history: what was successful yesterday will not necessarily be successful tomorrow, and the companies that anticipate tomorrow will be the ones that prevail—even if it means disrupting their business today. Netflix began in 1997 as an online DVD rental company, packing the discs in red envelopes and mailing them through the US Postal Service. Blockbuster, the video store juggernaut, entered the same online DVD delivery business in 2004. Then, in 2007, Netflix saw the digital future and introduced its streaming business, and with a more convenient and better product, that offering steadily grew at the expense of DVD rental sales. Seemingly overnight, an obscure video rental business became a cultural force. Netflix now has 125 million streaming subscribers worldwide. It generates award-winning original content, and it even retained its DVD rental service business (it just devised an app for it). Its market capitalization is more than $150 billion. Blockbuster, on the other hand, either didn't see the future or refused to adapt to it. At its peak in 2004, it had 9,000 stores in the

United States alone, but consumer preferences, for downloads, streaming, and binge watching, were about to shift. Each brick-and-mortar outlet proved to be a millstone on the balance sheet, and Blockbuster had no viable alternatives. The company filed for bankruptcy protection in 2010. It began shutting down its stores, and by 2018, only about a dozen remained open in the United States, with its original laminated membership cards selling as collector items on eBay for $11.99 apiece.

Netflix had the courage to reinvent itself, and flourished. Blockbuster didn't, and died.

Convulsive change has always been part of capitalism, but technology and globalization have accelerated the shocks. Artificial intelligence alone could have the same effect, in both economic and social change, that electricity or computers once had. All manner of companies across all kinds of business, from manufacturing to finance, from publishing to retail, adhere to business models that may soon be obsolete, if they aren't already.

Who wins and who loses? It starts with the courage to challenge the status quo, even if that displeases existing stakeholders or puts the business itself at short-term risk. The role of the CEO is to paint a clear picture of what the future holds, and that includes an honest assessment of the company's capabilities, a catalog of the changes necessary to be relevant tomorrow, and a willingness to make the difficult decisions to proceed.

That was our mind-set at Aetna. During our negotiations with CVS, my board asked me why we should sell a company that was performing so well and was delivering to its customers and its shareholders.

I told them that it wasn't about the past or even the present, but it was about the future, and the future of health care is a huge unknown. No one likes the system. Big insurers are routinely blamed for its ills, and we don't know what changes or reforms are coming that could dramatically change our business model. I also told the board that I believe our health care system is fundamentally broken, and all the players involved—hospitals, providers, drug and device companies, regulators, and insurers—fight to maintain a status quo from which they are benefiting. While Aetna has figured out how to prosper in that system, we should be leading the inevitable change, not responding to it.

"If we're not influencing health care and are just paying claims," I said, "we're dead."

Skeptics of the CVS deal understandably wondered how we could truly transform such an ossified, complicated system. We've been receiving health care the same way for so many decades, it takes some moxie—or maybe blind faith—to imagine that it could be done any other way.

I have absolutely no illusions about how difficult the task will be, but I'm tired of people talking endlessly about "health care reform," drafting white papers, holding conferences, and expressing dismay. It's time to act. If leadership means anything, it means seizing the moment, embracing a bold strategy to solve big problems, and executing on it. That's what the CVS deal was all about. It may take a generation, but it's an opportunity to redefine how we deliver care and reconsider the very meaning of health and wellness.

For the effort to succeed, the implementation will be critical. A thousand details will have to be monitored, and you'll need a maniac with the focus, the tenacity, and the urgency to resolve them all.

I won't be that maniac. There was only room for one

CEO, and Larry Merlo was it. He had the bigger balance sheet, and his is the acquiring company; so he deserves to lead the new organization. If the Humana deal had gone through, I probably would have been in that spot, and I would have relished the opportunity. But that's not how the cards played out. I could have maintained Aetna as an independent company and continued as its CEO, but it's not about me or my legacy, and it's not about what my predecessors had built. It's about the future, and I know that Aetna itself—the name, the brand, the products—will continue to thrive under the CVS umbrella. My senior leaders are now part of the new management team, and they will take what they've built at Aetna and help CVS reach new heights.

I spent fifteen years at Aetna, and I consider my departure one more example of how sometimes leaders have to lose attachments for the greater good. It may hurt, but it was the right thing to do. New challenges await.

13

WHEN BEST INTENTIONS ARE NOT ENOUGH

EVERYONE VALUES CREATIVE THINKING AND SMART strategies, but those rarely determine the success or failure of any given program or initiative. The outcome depends on execution—on the organization's ability to get on its belly, crawl through the mud, and carry out the mission effectively. That's even more true when the organization is doing something ambitious. It's about building the right model, testing it, and learning from the mistakes, and then doing it all over again.

Build, test, learn.

Build, test, learn.

It has to be a fast cycle, it's not always exciting, and it forces the leader to adjust, improvise, and, when necessary, abandon something that's not working. That's not easy when the cause is noble. Sometimes your efforts bring about real and lasting change, but other times, even your best intentions are not enough.

FEW CHALLENGES IN American life are more fraught than end-of-life care: how do you care for a loved one who is dying, in a way that demonstrates compassion but does not impose unnecessary physical and financial costs? Extending life is deeply personal, yet it has profound social implications, and we as a country have avoided addressing them.

On average, people spend 60 percent of their lifetime health care costs in the last six months of their life. What often happens is family members sit in the waiting room, urging the doctors to do something, and the doctors, playing savior, oblige with procedures or tests that often have little value and are usually painful, but they generate costs that are unsustainable for the payers. It's the worst of both worlds: higher costs for the system, and more discomfort for the patient.

Hospice care offers a different option—and I know the advantages and disadvantages from Eric's experiences. On the one hand, hospice care is far more humane (in Eric's case, a more comfortable room and a cessation of painful interventions). Hospice care is also paid by Medicare, which is obviously attractive to the hospital or any hospice provider. But under Medicare's reimbursement rules, once you enter hospice care, you have to forgo all curative services and acknowledge that you will die in six months. This is precisely why we delayed moving Eric to the hospice for as long as possible. We didn't want to admit that he had reached the end. The system creates a terrible choice for patients, which is why so many of them languish in the ICU and are subjected to stressful, unnecessary, and expensive procedures.

With these experiences in mind, I became part of a team at Aetna that assessed end-of-life care, and I suggested that we do something completely different. Let's tell our members: You can choose hospice care but still receive curative treatment. In other words, you don't have to admit that you're going to die in six months. If a miracle drug comes along, you can still be saved. We conducted a two-year study giving patients this option, and the number of people who chose hospice care increased to 74 percent from 24 percent; hospital days in inpatient beds decreased by 89 percent, and costs declined by 78 percent.

The results were entirely predictable. Of course, people chose the more humane, more comfortable hospice setting, including their own home, knowing they could still receive curative services. What was less predictable was that people in hospice care *lived longer*. Spared unnecessary procedures, they had less stress and a better quality of life. According to our results, conventional therapy shortened lives. Compassionate care lengthened lives.

Aetna has been offering Compassionate Care to all its members since 2010. Each year we analyze the program and amend it, and we work hard to implement it effectively. The result: We've taken something that Medicare pays for (about $12.5 billion a year for hospice care), and we've said we can do it better so we'll pay for it ourselves.

This option should be available to everyone, and we thought we had a good chance of expanding it beyond Aetna.

When the Obama administration held hearings on the Affordable Care Act in 2010, I presented our Compassionate Care data demonstrating the opportunity to save the health care system billions of dollars and to greatly improve the quality of life for patients at the end of life. The administration said I needed to gather the nation's hospice leaders and hold a conference at the Institute of Medicine, which would then issue a recommendation. I did, and the hospice leaders loved our approach. But it wasn't that easy. Encouraging patients to go to hospice care raised the specter of Sarah Palin's death panels. During the conference, Ezekiel Emanuel, one of the ACA's architects, announced, "This is a political time bomb. We can't do this."

I tried to explain that our program was *optional*—our members are free to receive traditional end-of-life care. No one is being forced into a hospice. There are no "death panels" or any other kind of panels. But the facts didn't matter. Every politician in America talks about the need to lower health care costs, but until we address end-of-life costs, substantive reductions will never happen.

We had the best intentions on how to address a seemingly intractable problem, and our program works for our members, but our proposal on how to save the system billions of dollars while improving quality of life at end of life sits on someone's bookcase, in someone's office, somewhere in Washington.

THE CONTROVERSIES surrounding end-of-life care are nothing compared to those that engulf the ACA, or Obamacare. The law itself was President Obama's signature domestic achievement, and its successes, shortcomings, and legacy will be hotly debated for generations to come. Aetna had an important role in this Washington battle that had implications for the entire country, and I briefly got caught in the crossfire.

Starting with my predecessor, Ron Williams, Aetna was heavily engaged with the ACA's creation. Ron spent countless hours in Washington to support a bill that would provide health coverage to uninsured Americans. The legislation would do so through policies sold by commercial insurers, with the assistance of government subsidies for low-income individuals and families. Medicaid would also be expanded to reach additional Americans. The essential goal of the ACA—universal coverage—looked a lot like Aetna's plan on Transforming Health Care in America, which was written in 2005. As a company, we were all in.

I was Aetna's CEO shortly after the time the ACA was passed in 2010, and I believed in the intent of the legislation just as strongly as Ron did. When the law was fully implemented in 2013 and 2014, Aetna was the ACA's single largest participant in the public exchanges, or the state-based online marketplaces where people could purchase individual health insurance policies. (The federal government operated its own online exchange for the states that did not want to build their own.) We were in fifteen states and would enroll 1 million people—no other commercial insurer had as big a footprint as we had, and no other commercial insurer was as fully committed. When the ACA's member-run health insurance co-op collapsed in Iowa, Aetna entered the market and saved the program.

I believed in the ACA philosophically. I knew the reality, from my childhood, of being one medical mishap away from financial ruin or of not having the resources for basic care. As noted, my mom worked part-time at the pediatrician's office so she could bring home the vaccines, and many families in our neighborhood had to find creative ways to secure health care. I didn't know it, but we were all at risk.

I also believed that the ACA made economic sense for Aetna. I looked at the public exchanges as new markets, in which we would enter fifteen. Entering any new market de novo incurs initial costs—about $50 million before the market stabilizes financially. If we had entered fifteen states unrelated to the ACA, it would have cost us about $750 million. Alternatively, if we had purchased 1 million new members, it would have cost us around $1,300 per member, or about

$1.3 billion. Losing money in the first two years of our ACA participation would not be alarming, because we expect to lose money when we enter new markets. But the losses were only acceptable if they led to stable returns over time, and our model assumed that by 2016, we would either be breaking even or making a profit.

Many assumptions that we made about the program, however—as well as about the administration and lawmakers—proved wrong.

The ACA legislation itself and its subsequent regulations represented one of the most complex pieces of social legislation in American history—the law was 2,300 pages, and the regulations were more than 20,000 pages. Even if they got everything right the first time, the administration or Congress would still need to amend the law or its regulations every year as market conditions changed or as different market dynamics emerged. That's what the federal government does for Medicare, Medicaid, and Social Security. If any one of those programs were left untouched for five years, it would collapse.

But that type of intervention and repair never happened with the ACA. From its inception, it lacked bipartisan support, and it became so toxic politically that neither the Obama administration nor Democratic lawmakers were willing to reopen and fix the problems that were manifest from day one—or before day one. (And I'm not even talking about the botched rollout of the federal government's website, which crashed two hours after its launch in October 2013.)

Almost immediately after passage and to win support for the law, President Obama announced that individual Americans could keep their own insurance, which meant they did not have to enter the public exchanges. But insurance is all about risk pools, in which healthier, less expensive individuals effectively subsidize those who are sicker and more expensive. Before the ACA was passed, individual insurance was typically available only to relatively healthy people. If they could keep their insurance and did not participate in the exchanges, the risk of the ACA pools would be excessively high. The ACA also needed uninsured healthy individuals to buy into the exchanges—the so-called mandate—but the penalties for failing to sign up were too low; thus many of these healthy individuals simply paid the fine and didn't enroll.

The risk pools never got the right mix of people, which led to higher premiums for participants and steeper losses for insurers. At its core, the ACA was about insurance reform, not health care reform, and it worked for those participants who were subsidized, but it was too expensive for almost everyone else.

There were other systemic problems. The Centers for Medicare and Medicaid Services, which oversees the ACA, adopted rules that permitted consumers to buy insurance during special enrollment periods outside of the annual open enrollment times, but this effectively allowed consumers to buy plans when they were sick and cancel them when they were healthy. Even worse, CMS didn't have the back-end systems to collect and analyze data, another huge failure. Our entire business runs on data, which are needed to determine everything from the eligibility of participants to the efficacy of programs, but CMS had no way to independently amass that information.

Then there were the scammers, or the people who figure out how to cheat the system. In what is called "the regulatory circumvention curve," it typically takes eighteen to twenty-four months to determine how to break the rules of any new law or regulation, and that's what happened with the ACA.

Dialysis, for example, was an area of rampant abuse. Medicare and Medicaid pay about $300 for one dialysis treatment, whereas the insurers on the exchanges paid almost $1,000. Dialysis companies gave money to the National Kidney Foundation to encourage Medicare and Medicaid dialysis patients to move to the exchanges—the foundation subsidized the premiums for those individuals. The commercial insurers, including Aetna, suddenly faced a surge in dialysis patients, and our costs skyrocketed. In another fraud, a hemophilia specialty pharmacy signed up forty of its patients as employees. This made them eligible for our small group product on the exchanges. It was an elaborate scheme—the patients even signed W2 forms. We eventually discovered it, but that one incident cost us $27 million.

We told CMS about these abuses and others, but the agency didn't have the systems or the expertise to stop them immediately; our unexpected costs continued to rise.

Congress also failed to fund programs that were supposed to protect insurers which had unexpectedly high claims. These were known as "risk-corridor payments." In 2014, insurers requested $2.87 billion, but CMS paid only $362 million. Aetna had requested $100 million but received only $12.5 million. CMS didn't allocate any risk-corridor payments in 2015 or 2016.

The federal reinsurance plan also didn't work out as designed. It was supposed to spread risk among the insurers so that those carriers that had healthier members and were making money would subsidize those that had sicker members and were losing money. Problem was, virtually all of us were losing money. Even though Aetna was experiencing losses, we still had to pay CMS money to assist those insurers who were losing even more money.

In our first two years on the exchanges, we lost $250 million. That was manageable, but the problems were not getting fixed. Doing so required hard work, adjustments, follow-up.

Build, test, learn.

Build, test, learn.

Instead, the approach was wait, watch, scramble.

Then came 2016, the year we thought we'd at least break even. We knew that wasn't going to happen, but on an earnings call in April, I said that we could continue to sustain manageable losses and expressed hope that the administration and Congress would repair the law. But our second quarter was a rout, and by June we saw that the risk pools were continuing to deteriorate, the abuses had not abated, and our losses were mounting. We also owed CMS $54 million for the reinsurance pool. We were now running projections for significant losses in 2016 and even greater losses in 2017. In light of that information, we disclosed that we were going to consider withdrawing from some of the state exchanges, though we had until August to determine which ones and to notify those states.

Shortly after that disclosure, we received a call from CMS, which had its own concerns. The 2016 election was around the corner, and the ACA was a centerpiece of President Obama's legacy. That meant Republicans wanted to see it fail, Democrats wanted to see it stabilized, and the Obama administration wanted to see it succeed. The perception of the law—was it a godsend or an albatross?—could influence which party controlled the Senate and indeed which party controlled the White House. The last thing CMS wanted to hear was that we were considering pulling out of certain markets, particularly in states with hotly contested US Senate races. My conversations with CMS focused more on short-term accommodations to keep us in the exchanges than on long-term solutions to repair the program. My discussions with members of Congress were no more productive. Most politicians enter public life with good intentions, but those intentions are often subordinated to the exigencies of maintaining power or keeping their job—and I saw that repeatedly with the ACA. It was too polarizing an issue to tolerate compromise or seek bipartisan support.

That put us in a bind. Given Aetna's extensive involvement in the Medicare Advantage and Medicaid programs, I have every incentive to accommodate both political parties, all branches of government, and every administration. But I always put the interests of our company first, and that position didn't satisfy any of the partisans in Washington. Whichever course we took would draw fire from someone.

In July 2016, we still had made no decisions about the exchanges, but our problems with the administration were just beginning.

The Department of Justice was in the midst of reviewing Aetna's proposed acquisition of Humana. In May, one of our outside lawyers told the DOJ that if the agency blocked the deal, Aetna was going to "pull out of all the exchanges." That was not our position—it was a misstatement—but it prompted a call in late June from the DOJ Antitrust Division, which wanted to talk to me on the phone about the comment. I didn't want to do a phone interview but offered to fly down and meet with the DOJ personally. The agency rejected that request and instead sent me a "civil investigation demand," or a letter asking me to answer several questions that centered on one issue: If the DOJ kills the Humana deal, what impact would that have on our participation in the exchanges?

On July 5, we sent the DOJ a three-page response. It explained the current financial problems with the exchanges but said that if the Humana deal proceeded without litigation, "we would explore how to devote a portion of the additional synergies . . . to supporting even more public exchange coverage over the next few years." The letter also said that if the Humana acquisition was blocked, Aetna would owe Humana a $1 billion breakup fee, and Aetna would also face significant unrecoverable costs, including carrying costs of the debt required to finance the deal. Aetna would incur as well significant litigation expenses should the DOJ sue Aetna.

Those unexpected costs would exceed $2 billion, and that would deplete our capital structure. It would also force us to cull our lowest-performing assets, one of which was our products on the exchanges. Given those facts, the letter said, if the DOJ sues Aetna to stop the Humana transaction, "we will immediately take action to reduce our 2017 exchange footprint." The letter said we would withdraw from five states and shelve plans to expand to five additional states.

The DOJ called me to testify on July 12, and one of the lawyers asked me if I was "threatening the Department of Justice" by saying we would reduce our footprint should the DOJ sue us.

"Absolutely not," I told him. I explained that if the Humana deal was blocked, the costs would be so high that we would be forced to pare our lowest-performing assets, "which is what every responsible businessperson would do."

The lawyer approached me after my testimony and apologized for asking the question, but he said it was his job.

The DOJ filed its lawsuit to block the merger on July 21, alleging that it would increase concentration in the insurance industry and harm competition across the country.

We were now going to have to defend ourselves in US

district court in Washington, but separate from the lawsuit, we also faced an August 5 deadline to inform the states about our plans for the exchanges. I was meeting with our senior executives every three days, and they were urging me to pull out of all fifteen states. It made the most sense financially as well as politically. If we left some states but remained in others, we'd be accused of playing politics or dispensing favors to certain governors or state lawmakers. It was smarter to just abandon all the markets and stop the bleeding. But if we got out of the exchanges entirely, it would be difficult to get back in, and I thought we should try to live for another day. We had emotional capital as well as financial capital in these products. We knew that lives would be affected, including our own employees. We had hired nine hundred people to work on the ACA, and their jobs would be threatened if we pulled out entirely. I concluded that we should stay in some markets and hope that the next administration—I assumed it would be Hillary Clinton's—could fix the problems.

I asked my team in what states could we remain to keep our 2017 losses under $1 billion, which I described as "the stupid mark."

We decided to stay in four markets in 2017—Delaware, Iowa, Nebraska, and Virginia—and withdraw from the other eleven. I hoped that would at least keep the door open for us to continue while keeping our losses under $1 billion.

About a week or so later, I received a call from someone at CMS, telling me that it had just received a Freedom of Information Act request from the *Huffington Post*. The publication asked for a copy of my July 5 letter responding to the DOJ's questions about what might happen if the Humana deal was killed.

"We're inclined to release the letter immediately," he told me.

"You guys take six months to a year to release anything," I said.

"Yes, but we're trying to improve our response rate for FOIAs."

Our decision to pull back from the exchanges had nothing to do with the DOJ's suit, but the two would now be conflated to embarrass us.

"Put what you want out there," I said. "I'll bear the pain."

The *Huffington Post* said our letter was a "clear threat" against the DOJ. NPR's headline read: "Aetna CEO to Justice Department: Block Our Deal and We'll Drop Out of Obamacare." The *Washington Times* said Aetna "threatened feds with Obamacare pullout." The online publication *Quartz* said Aetna had used Obamacare as a "hostage" in negotiating with the government. My picture was prominently displayed on most of these stories. The basis of our decision—the investments we had made in the exchanges, the losses we had incurred, the additional losses that we were projecting, and the financial impact of a DOJ lawsuit—was mostly ignored.

During the trial, we learned that CMS, the DOJ, and the White House were in communication with one another regarding our involvement in the ACA. We thought the different government branches were supposed to be independent of each other, but the system doesn't work that way.

My team was correct in one regard. Pulling out of all fifteen markets, instead of eleven, would have been much easier to explain and might have made a difference in the lawsuit. The DOJ alleged that the merger would lessen competition in the exchanges in seventeen counties in Florida, Georgia, and

Missouri. But Aetna had already announced that it was leaving those markets! The merger could not reduce competition in those markets if only one of us—Humana—was in them.

But in January 2017, Judge John Bates ruled in favor of the DOJ and blocked the merger. As I've already noted, one issue pertained to whether Medicare competed against Medicare Advantage. The other central issue revolved around those seventeen counties. According to Judge Bates, Aetna had withdrawn from those counties "to improve its litigation position." The judge accepted our view that we would not be competing in Georgia and Missouri "in the near future," but he wrote that "Aetna is likely to compete in Florida after 2017"—which, if true, would justify blocking the merger to preserve having two competing insurers in that state.

By 2018, Aetna had withdrawn from all public exchanges in all states, including Florida.

THE FEDERAL GOVERNMENT touches every company, so no business leader can ignore it. Attention must always be paid. But as our experiences with the ACA and the Humana transaction reminded me, leaders must also be realistic. The arguments that you present in the marketplace—the evidence that you adduce, the analysis that you offer, the outcomes that you project—rarely receive the same hearing in Washington. The objectives there, often geared to the next election, are simply different. So, you make your best case and prepare for Plan B.

The ACA survives, despite efforts by President Trump and congressional Republicans to kill it. The media usually report on how many people sign up each year, and in 2018, 11.8 million people enrolled, which was a slight decline from 2017. (That number does not include people who gained coverage through the ACA's expansion of Medicaid.) The consensus is that the exchanges are "stable." But the program's original goal was to provide coverage for all uninsured Americans—universal coverage—and we still have about 28 million people uninsured, primarily because the cost of coverage is too high. The law never came close to achieving its actual objective, and its future seems uncertain: The Republican Congress has repealed the penalties for individuals who go without insurance, which will further deter enrollment of the very people needed to sustain the program. And that seems to be the plan.

In 2018, the Trump administration proposed new rules to allow small businesses to band together to create health plans that sidestep many ACA requirements—the plans offer lower costs but fewer benefits. That means they will attract healthier members, further weakening the exchanges. The administration also cut millions of dollars for nonprofit insurance counselors, known as navigators, who helped people obtain ACA coverage. What President Trump could not destroy by law he is seeking to eliminate through sabotage.

There was, in my view, a simpler way to achieve a better result. If the government had lowered the age of Medicare to fifty-five and means-tested the benefits, and if it had offered the Medicaid expansion to all the states, it would have enlarged two programs that are already working well, covered the same number of people (if not more), and done so at a fraction of the cost of the ACA. I also supported the market stabilization package—sponsored by Senators Lamar Alexander and Patty Murray—that would have funded the ACA's subsidies for three years, funded three years of federal reinsurance at $10 billion a year, and added ACA waiver flexibility to the states. But in March 2018, that bipartisan effort collapsed over a debate about federal funding of abortion.

Even under its current provisions, Obamacare could have covered more people at less cost had its operational and design problems been confronted and fixed. No matter how inspiring the vision or lofty the goals, success or failure always comes down to execution.

The ACA highlighted that the deeper you wade into the political world, the less control you have and the more exposed you leave your organization. The obstacles created by government can be so significant that sometimes companies just have to do it on their own. Our Compassionate Care program works because we control it, we make the adjustments every year, and we crawl through the mud to ensure its success.

We had the best intentions with the ACA, but that wasn't enough.

The experience reminds me of something that the Dalai Lama once said. He was at a board meeting for the Mind & Life Institute, a nonprofit that promotes contemplative sciences and practices. Mari and I were there, and someone asked the Dalai Lama, "If you are threatened physically and you fear for your safety, how should you feel toward that person, and what is the right response?"

The Dalai Lama said, "You must always hold in your heart compassion for any living thing, because in that compassion you find love. Mentally, you must find compassion. But physically, you run away."

There was silence. Then Mari said, "You mean, 'Lovingly, run away'?"

"Yes," the Dalai Lama said. "Lovingly, run away."

That's how I feel about the Affordable Care Act. I wanted to make it work, but I couldn't, and I was putting our company at risk by staying in it.

Lovingly, I ran away.

14

THE MIRACLE ON 134TH STREET

IN 1697, A BAND OF CANADIAN INDIANS LAID SIEGE TO
Haverhill, Massachusetts, a small town near the New Hampshire border. More than twenty-five residents were killed,
and the Indians left the burning village with a number of
hostages, including Hannah Duston, whose newborn son was
among the dead. (The Indians killed the males and took the
women and girls.) The captives were forced to walk forty-
five miles along the Merrimack River, until one night, when
Hannah took revenge. She slayed her captors in their sleep
and returned triumphantly with their scalps. The Massachusetts General Assembly awarded her fifty pounds.

The episode of frontier justice has been memorialized by
such luminaries as Cotton Mather, who transformed Hannah into a Puritan saint, and later by Nathaniel Hawthorne,
John Greenleaf Whittier, and Henry David Thoreau. In 1879,
Haverhill (pronounced HAY-vrill) commissioned a bronze
statue of Hannah, grasping a tomahawk with one hand and
scalps with the other, and there it stands today, in Grand Army
Park (though the tomahawk and the scalps were removed a
number of years ago).

I have a personal interest in Hannah Duston. She is my
great-great-great-aunt on my mother's side, and perhaps I
inherited some of her survival instincts. Her story has been
widely interpreted over the years and has also generated

controversy—critics have said that it's been used to justify our shameful treatment of Indians—but I'm more struck by Hannah's appeal. It is surely about vengeance, justice, and heroism, but it's also about community: she returned to Haverhill and became a dramatic symbol for how neighbors defend themselves and resurrect a devastated town.

It's an extreme example, but it highlights for me how we have always made community central to our lives. I've already argued that we need to bring health care back to the community, but this reorientation is about much more than health. Our country has continued to grow in population (we now have more than 325 million Americans) and has become more heterogeneous and more complex, and our response has been to create larger governmental entities. Those models no longer work, and the American people recognize that. In 2018, the Pew Research Center released a poll showing that only 20 percent of adults surveyed believe that democracy is working "very well" in the United States, while 67 percent believe that "significant changes" are needed to "governmental design and structure."

Commenting in the *New York Times*, Neil Gross, a professor of sociology, suggested that these results would not have surprised some of our earliest political thinkers, who advocated for smaller units of government. "Plato and Aristotle," Gross wrote, "admired the city-state because they thought reason and virtue could prevail only when a polis was small enough that citizens could be acquaintances," and Montesquieu argued that " 'in a large republic, the common good is sacrificed to a thousand considerations,' whereas in a smaller one, the common good 'is more strongly felt, better known, and closer to each citizen.' "

Those lessons have not been applied to our age, as our leaders seem to believe that we can impose rules and regulations from above on an increasingly diverse population that wants increasingly different things. I am not making a big government–small government political argument. What I am saying is that people live in cities, they live in counties, they live in school districts, they live in neighborhoods anchored by local institutions. We've already seen, in the political world, communities trying to take control of their own destinies. After the Trump administration announced it was going to withdraw from the Paris Agreement on climate change, more than 400 cities and more than 100 companies, including Aetna, announced that they were going to adhere to the deal. This was huge. It said that change can and will happen at the local level, and if this change can be done for the environment, it can surely be done for other matters.

Whatever the issue, I believe that to affect people's lives, we need nimble organizations that are on the ground and responsive to the particular needs of people within those boundaries.

Take our country's obesity crisis. We all recognize the problem, and we bandy about national numbers from the federal government that document its severity. (For the record, nearly 40 percent of adult Americans are now obese, and our military has been rejecting increasing numbers of applicants because they are overweight.) But those national numbers provide little help in actual treatment and prevention because we don't have one obesity problem. We have, instead, many obesity problems across the country. The obesity rates in say, Palm Springs, California, are different from those in T pelo, Mississippi, and all the factors that contribute to we

gain—the built environment, food "deserts," socioeconomic status, genetics—vary widely between these two communities, and they vary among all communities. Whether it's obesity, poverty, illiteracy, mental illness, declining labor force participation, tainted water, opioids, or any other social ill—you name it—the programs with the highest likelihood of success are those that are developed locally. The programs may need money or other resources from the outside, but the communities themselves have to be invested in their design and results.

Just as I've tried to delegate authority at Aetna to those who are closest to our members, I believe we need to do the same thing with our governmental, civic, and nonprofit organizations. In short, be local. I further contend that our country's future hinges on our ability to restore, revive, and strengthen our communities. Granted, that's a bit like standing for motherhood and apple pie—everyone favors "community" in the abstract. But as corporate leaders, we need to demonstrate what that means in reality.

WHEN I BECAME president of Aetna, I also became chairman of the Aetna Foundation, which is funded each year by company profits. The foundation itself was created in 1972, but Aetna's commitment to civic and charitable causes is as old as the company itself, with an emphasis on education, health care, and the arts. Since 1980, Aetna and the Aetna Foundation have contributed more than $465 million in grants and sponsorships.

However, when I became the foundation's leader, I thought we needed to be more goal oriented and tied more directly to Aetna's mission of making the world a healthier place; specifi-

cally, I wanted to focus on the narrowing of racial and ethnic health disparities. To assist in that effort, I hired Dr. Garth Graham, a cardiologist who had been a deputy assistant secretary at the US Department of Health and Human Services in the Bush and Obama administrations, where he also ran the Office of Minority Health. When I interviewed Garth, he started telling me about his resume, and I cut him short.

"Don't worry about that," I said. "What I want to know is, if you could do anything you could to change the world, what would that look like?"

Garth talked about different ways to lessen poverty, including access to food and the power of community gardens—both as a source of nutrition and a symbol of change. He talked about using technology and crowdsourcing and other strategies to engage people in their own health. It was clear that we saw the world in the same way. Our discussion centered on how to motivate communities to address some of their most important health needs, and what role the Aetna Foundation could play in that process.

That was the genesis of the Healthiest Cities & Counties Challenge, cosponsored with the American Public Health Association and the National Association of Counties. The Aetna Foundation issued a request to small- and mid-sized cities for innovative solutions to urgent public health issues. Frankly, we were not expecting that many submissions because our actual financial offer was small—an initial $10,000 planning grant. To our surprise, we had 400 cities apply, and in 2016 we chose the 50 most promising proposals.

We tried to create incentives so if the programs gained traction, the cities could receive an additional $25,000 and, for dramatic improvements, up to $1.5 million over two years. Several of our winning cities submitted proposals about safety in general and gun violence in particular. Kansas City, Missouri, proposed to understand gun violence as we understand disease: if we can identify risk factors for, say, type 2 diabetes, cardiac disease, or cancer, we can intervene and reduce those risks. The same is true for gun violence. If we can identify the risk factors that lead to homicide—anger, distrust, insecurity, isolation—and if we can intervene with mindfulness or social work, then maybe we can deescalate those risks before the trigger is pulled. Let's see how the program does over time, but it's a novel approach to gun violence, and it's time we start thinking differently about it.

The connection between physical safety and personal health cannot be overstated. If residents don't feel safe to walk the streets, ride their bikes, or go to the park, that community's physical and mental health will suffer. The problems are complex, but even small gestures can be meaningful. For example, we've been gathering health data in Baltimore for many years, and one time I joined our team in talking to community leaders.

They said they wanted to "take back their streets."

I asked them what their biggest problem was.

They said their relationship with police.

I said, "Why don't you take a police officer on a walk?"

That led to a program, funded in part by the Aetna Foundation, that involves police officers going door-to-door, meeting with residents, and taking walks with them. Has that made every street corner in Baltimore safe? Of course not, but anything that promotes trust between the police and the citizens is a step forward in creating a stronger community.

Our Healthiest Cities & Counties Challenge has taught us that initiatives don't have to be splashy or expensive to make a difference. In Allentown, Pennsylvania, for example, we funded an exercise program that was initially launched as part of the CDC's Million Hearts Initiative. Allentown's goal was simple—get more people walking. The program uses ten "job clocks," which are typically used for construction workers to punch in. But Allentown set them up on park trails and gave residents key tabs to punch in when they completed a walk. The city records every click, and each month, Allentown has a random prize drawing—a twenty-five-dollar gift card—for one of its walkers. About 2,400 people are involved in the program.

Walking is something that most able-bodied people can do, but some other incentive is needed beyond abstract appeals to health. Allentown figured that out.

"Once people saw each other clicking, it really caught on," said Tina Amado, the nutrition and physical activity manager at the Allentown Health Bureau. "It's social, it instills community pride, and I think people just feel as if they are part of this greater whole."

For all the talk about the "unraveling of the social fabric," I believe the desire to tighten that fabric is quite strong. Camden, New Jersey, had sewers backing up during heavy rains, sending sewage into parks, homes, and waterways and spreading the risk of infection. Through our challenge, we funded an initiative that would expand existing efforts to build green infrastructure projects, including rain gardens, tree plantings, and large cisterns used to collect rainwater. In addition, residents can notify the authorities, through a website, of any flooding or illegal dumping of trash. Mobile apps and social media are used as well to communicate with residents about floods. While these efforts are now supported by the city, county, and state, they began with neighborhood organizations and nonprofits coming together to combat the floods.

Whether our challenge program has given money to "Little Havana" Miami to increase health access; to Wichita Falls, Texas, to reduce secondhand smoke; or to Avondale, Arizona, to increase recreational programs for children, these efforts are working because they came from those communities. As a doctor, Garth Graham noted that compliance rates with prescriptions are often low because they are "prescriptive"—an injunction from a health care provider to do something. When it comes to health, he said, a better approach is to have ideas "bubble up" from the bottom. "If you allow people to make the decisions that motivate them the most, that creates the most sustainable change," he said. "We denigrate about what motivates us—we assume that we are motivated financially. But what really motivates us is making our families better and then our communities better, and then hopefully the world."

Mari and I have created our own foundation, called Anahata (or "heart chakra," which is associated with balance and serenity). It was largely funded by the many shares of stock that I had accumulated at Aetna. Those shares represented a significant portion of our compensation, and I held them until I retired, with one exception (I sold a bloc as part of my divorce settlement). I obviously believed in our corporate strategy, but I thought it was still important that my financial interests were aligned directly with those of our shareholders. I'm grateful that most of my wealth will go to our foundation, which will be used to invest in community and rural development.

In some ways, Mari and I run our foundation as my team and I ran Aetna. I can't be on the ground and making decisions for those nonprofit organizations or charitable groups that receive our money, but I want to be involved. I want to

know what's going on. I want to believe in their m

when possible or appropriate, I want to offer sugg

ideas. That's what happened with Tony Hillery, wh

ning life story is a reminder of why we all need to rol

sleeves and get our fingernails dirty.

EACH YEAR AETNA produces an African American caler
which features a different leader for each month, and we h
an event that celebrates the calendar. In 2014, the event w
held in St. Louis and was dedicated to urban farmers acro
America. Mari is an experienced community gardener and i
always encouraging me to grow tomatoes outside my office
window. So, I invited Mari to join me in St. Louis, where
she'd meet fellow gardeners.

At one point, I took the stage and sat next to two of the
urban farmers featured in the calendar. One was Tony Hillery, who is the founder of Harlem Grown. In making small
talk, I turned to him and asked, "Tony, how does it feel to be
Mr. February?"

"It feels great," he said, "but when I go back to New York,
I'll be dealing with the same stuff I left yesterday. Nothing has
changed because I'm in the calendar."

"What do you propose to do about that?" I asked him.

"Honestly, if we had some more partners, we could make
a big change," he said. "I really think we're onto something."

When we got off the stage, I introduced Tony to Mari,
who said, "You're in Harlem? We're near Harlem also!" (We
have a place on the Upper West Side.) They had a long conversation about Harlem Grown, which began in 2011 as an
urban farm for elementary students.

On a Saturday morning some months later, Mari and I rode our bikes up to the farm, on 134th Street between Malcolm X Boulevard and Adam Clayton Powell Jr. Boulevard, and started working, planting, and talking to the kids. It was demanding labor, but everyone was focused, inspired, and connected. There was something special about this place, and about Tony.

HE DIDN'T GROW UP in a deprived home, but he knew deprivation soon enough.

Born in 1959, Tony was raised in Queens with a strong role model in his father, a Tuskegee airman who was shot down behind enemy lines during the Korean War; he received a Purple Heart from President Eisenhower and later joined the New York City Fire Department. Tony had seven siblings, and they all attended private school, but Tony became the self-described black sheep of the family. He dropped out of high school and started drinking and using drugs. At twenty-one he got married, and he and his wife soon had a girl, Toni, and they moved in with Tony Hillery's parents. One day Tony got into a fight with his wife and, as he described it, "put my hands on her." She called the police, who came to the house with a protection order.

Tony assumed his parents would tell his wife that she would have to leave. Instead, they told him that *he* would have to leave.

Tony now found himself unemployed and homeless, and at night, he slept on the subway trains. After a certain hour, the trains would stop, and one night he was sleeping on the F train laid up at Coney Island. It was cold, and when the lights flickered on and Tony woke up, he had blood on his hands

and legs. Someone had cut his jeans and stolen what was in the pocket while leaving him with gashes.

"Talk about fear," he later told me. "You're all alone. You're cold. You don't have your bearings, and you're covered in blood. That feeling will never leave. That's when I hit bottom."

He returned home and asked his father for help. They had a summer home in Sag Harbor on Long Island, and Tony settled in, found a job, joined AA, got sober, and slowly rebuilt his life. His marriage ended, but in time he returned to live and work in New York and discovered that he had an entrepreneurial streak. He opened a shoe repair business on the Upper East Side—"the only black-owned business as far as the eye could see"—and also opened a barbershop in Queens, sold it, and tripled his money. He was a UPS driver as well, delivering packages on the West Side, but after ten years and two knee surgeries, he left UPS and started driving for a limousine company. There he found an unlikely calling.

The company had an account with NBC, so the limos would pick up guests for the *Today* show, *Saturday Night Live,* and *Late Night with Conan O'Brien.* Tony had never driven anyone anywhere, but he found himself ferrying around celebrities—Robert Urich was one of his first. Tony developed such a strong rapport with Urich that the actor requested Tony be his driver every time he came to New York. Tony was assigned to other celebrities. He drove Cameron Diaz around for two weeks, including some eighteen-hour days to accommodate a busy social calendar.

By the middle 1990s, Tony was remarried, to Mary, and had two more children, Zachary and Raechel, and they were living in a nice home in Queens. The limousine company pushed Tony for more and more hours, and one day it called him to pick up an *SNL* host—it might have been Jennifer Lopez—and Tony refused because of exhaustion. The owner, who was white, called him "an ungrateful nigger."

That ended Tony's arrangement with the company and, Tony assumed, his career as a limo driver. But weeks later, he was at home and got a call from Robert Urich: he was coming to New York tomorrow, and he wanted Tony to pick him up.

"Bob, I'm not driving anymore," Tony said.

"That's what they told me at the company," Urich said. "I don't care. I need you."

"I don't have a car."

"I don't care. Get a bicycle if you have to! I'll see you at the airport."

And he hung up.

Tony went to Avis, rented a green minivan with cloth seats, and pulled up to meet Urich at the airport.

"Nice wheels," he told Tony, and Tony drove him for a full week.

Tony saw an opportunity. In 1999 he started his own limo business, TZR Transportation, named after his three children. He only worked on referrals—no website, no advertising, no marketing. He had a three-hour minimum, and he specialized in the rich and famous. He drove Janet Jackson, Chris Rock, and Stevie Wonder. Other clients included Tom Hanks, Nicole Kidman, and Keanu Reeves. There were NBA stars, rock stars, and film stars. Matt Damon told Tony to pick up an Armani suit for himself, Armani being one of Damon's sponsors. Many of the celebrities gave Tony swag, and to this day Tony's closet has all kinds of jackets and suits in which the tags have never been removed. When the Trump International Hotel and Tower opened in 1996, Tony was there, in Columbus Circle, dropping off and picking up, and he returned frequently.

Tony's secret was that he treated the A-listers as regular people, using his natural warmth to form bonds. Limo drivers are notorious snitches, paid off by gossip columnists or Internet trolls to divulge where their boldface clients are staying, dining, meeting with, or sleeping with. Tony could put his customers at ease, but he also asked questions—not about their latest project but about their family: "How's your mother doing?" "How's your wife?" "Where are you taking the kids for Christmas?" After each ride, he'd scribble notes so he'd remember family names, vacation spots, and personal details, and when he picked up that person the next time, he could ask those same questions but in a more personal manner.

"People are people," Tony said. "They have the same human needs." Even a big limo is confined space, and either you connect or you don't. It got to the point where his clients were asking Tony to pick up their mother at the airport. "I'd charge a premium for that," he said.

Tony's company had six cars and drew upon sixty drivers, and business continued to boom until the economy crashed in 2008. He had always relied on credit lines, but now they dried up. The agencies that paid his invoices took longer to respond. The Hollywood junkets that had always sent him passengers declined. Bookings fell. He couldn't get new cars. Insurance bills piled up. By now he and Mary had sold their home and were living in a beautiful condo on the Hudson, and by 2011, Tony was at another crossroads. He still had his business, but he was feeling depressed, spending his days on the couch playing video games. He knew his triggers that could return him to drugs and alcohol.

"I had to do something," he said.

He had been reading about schools, and he thought that might be where he should direct his attention. He looked on a subway map and saw that the No. 2 train stopped at 135th and Lenox (also Malcolm X Boulevard), and within a block of that stood PS 175, which was prekindergarten to fifth grade. Never mind that Tony himself was a high school dropout and had never set foot in a public school. He went to PS 175 and asked to see the principal.

"I'm here to help," he told her.

"Help with what?"

"I don't know, but I'd like to work with parents," he said.

He met with some of the parents and came to recognize true generational poverty. Eighty percent of the children in the school came from single-parent households; 92 percent lived below the poverty line; 98 percent were on food stamps; 42 percent were in homeless shelters. The parents themselves didn't even realize the condition they were in. "Mr. Tony," one mother told him, "why do you sweat this education stuff. I'm doing great." She lived in public housing and was on welfare and food stamps.

After three weeks, Tony decided to focus on the children and was assigned to the cafeteria. Two lunch periods, two hundred children at a time, running, yelling, pushing, jumping on tables. It was chaos. It was also essential. Some students came to school not just for reading, writing, and arithmetic but also for breakfast, lunch, and dinner.

The students didn't have creative outlets—no outdoor space for recess—so Tony started a recycling effort. He bought the students green T-shirts and gloves, called them "the Green Team," assigned table captains, and got the kids to sort trash, recycle, and compost. It was an important first step.

Tony had nicknames for all the students, and special handshakes, and he would go table to table and talk to the kids. With his shaved head, goatee, and black-framed glasses, he was an authority figure but also a soothing presence. One day he sat down next to a girl in kindergarten. She said she didn't like the cafeteria food, so she was eating some kind of sodium-processed snack, which she had brought from home and—according to the girl—it was a healthy option.

That led to a conversation about other kinds of food, like fruits and vegetables, and Tony asked her if she knew where tomatoes came from.

Of course she knew. She said they come from Pathmark, the grocery store.

Tony thought she was making a joke, but she was serious. *Tomatoes come from Pathmark!* She saw them on the vine, and she saw the mist and heard the sound of thunder, and she was certain that's where tomatoes came from.

Tony started to laugh. The girl started to cry. *Why is Mr. Tony making fun of me?* So, Tony walked around the cafeteria and asked the other kids where vegetables came from. Some knew about tomatoes and carrots, but not much more.

It was a terrible epiphany. As Tony later said, "They don't know what food is."

And why would they? In a three-block radius of the school, Tony counted fifty-four fast-food restaurants, twenty-nine pharmacies, and no affordable food options. "Generational poverty is not just one thing," he said. "It's behavioral. It's environmental. It's in your DNA. How do we break that?"

The answer: grow your own vegetables. Across the street from the school was an abandoned community garden, which the kids called "the haunted garden," overrun by weeds, rodents, car parts, and vagrants. He asked the city if he could take it over, and the city obliged.

Tony continued working in the cafeteria, but he otherwise devoted his time to cleaning up the garden, and when the school day ended, students joined him. He needed money to turn this into an urban farm, and he raised it from some of his limo clients and from the owner of a New Jersey auto dealership from which he had bought many cars. The garden dirt was contaminated, so Tony hired a landscaper to bring in fresh soil. He bought four hundred damaged seedlings from Home Depot, and the school had a big ceremony in which each student planted his or her own seedling. Now the kids had something to water and nurture, and they raced over to the garden after school to see how much their plant had grown. When they began to leaf in late May, the kids pulled off the greenery and ate it.

It was a miracle on 134th Street.

"When these kids saw something green at lunch, they'd throw it in the trash, and they'd eat something starchy and wash it down with chocolate milk," Tony said. "Now I have as a scientific fact: If they plant it, they will eat it."

Tony founded Harlem Grown and, with the help of Ed Norton, the actor and social activist who was one of Tony's limo clients, turned it into a 501(c)(3) nonprofit. (Ed sits on the board and helped secure $20,000 from the city.) But Tony is an entrepreneur, so he wanted to expand and diversify Harlem Grown. Near the garden, next to an empty tenement, lay another vacant lot, owned by the city's Department of Housing Preservation and Development. The lot hadn't been used in forty-two years. Tony asked if he could use the land, and when the agency agreed, Tony brought in seven tons of gravel and built a hydroponic greenhouse, equipped with pumps and a drainage system. The greenhouse operates year-round.

Just growing the vegetables, however, wasn't enough. "We

had our first crop of chard, and I sent it home with the kids," Tony said. "They came back the next day, and I said, 'How was that chard?' And they said, 'I don't know. My mom threw it away.'"

Tony needed to offer education and cooking classes, and he also had to support an urban farm as well as a hydroponic garden. He had to raise more money, and that led to another revelation.

Harlem Grown is a compelling story: impoverished kids growing the very foods—kale, chard, cabbage, collard greens—that the community itself does not provide, and those children using the vegetables to feed themselves and distribute to others. Tony himself is an inspiring apostle of community development. He connects with children on the margins of society, with compassion and empathy, in the same way that he connects with the Hollywood elite. Word spread of his efforts in Harlem, and volunteers from across the city began to show up.

Companies also offered their support. One was PwC, the large accounting and consulting firm. Several of its employees had volunteered at the garden and told their bosses about it. Executives emailed Tony and said the company wanted to give Harlem Grown a check for $10,000; it would be delivered in a presentation ceremony at the farm itself. On the morning of the ceremony, two limos pulled up, and some guys in business suits stepped out. A photo crew was already there. They wanted the kids to line up in front of the Harlem Grown sign, and the executives would hand over a big foam check with $10,000 written across it.

They expressed no interest in actually seeing the garden, and Tony concluded that they would have rather been anywhere else but Harlem Grown. He told the executives that he didn't want their money. "It might make them feel good," he later said, "but what did they actually do? They wrote a check, but they didn't change these kids' lives one bit. Money might buy gloves and rakes and other stuff, but they break and can be replaced. The kids are in the same spot."

It was a similar reaction that Tony had for me when Aetna put him on our calendar. A nice gesture, but it doesn't really change anything.

The PwC executives were rebuffed, but they returned a few days later to find out what went wrong. Tony explained that it's not just financial capital that he needs—it's human capital. It's role models. It's community leaders. Ask the younger children at Harlem Grown about college, and they'll say, "What's that?" Ask the older children about college, and they'll say, "Why?" Ask them about careers, and the boys will say they want to be LeBron, and the girls will say they want to be Beyoncé.

PwC got the message, and it began sending a group of employees to the farm every other weekend. Google wanted Tony to apply for a $100,000 grant. Tony refused, but Google is also sending volunteers to the farm. "Now my kids want to be coders," Tony said.

Harlem Grown is currently in six elementary schools, with mentors who offer mediation training and conflict resolution skills. It runs a summer camp and offers cooking classes to children as well as adults. It has a full-time staff of fifteen— "all college-educated women from the best schools in the country," Tony said—and it hires interns who have criminal records. "They work on the farm," he said. "We teach them being on time, being in uniform, being present, accepting constructive criticism, following through on tasks, the basics that we think everyone has, but they don't. We're teaching them how to work."

The goal is to break the poverty-to-prison pipeline. The interns who excel are hired for paying jobs—six or seven dollars above minimum wage—and to get paid, they have to open a checking account for automatic transfers. Financial literacy is part of the program. They also learn about emails and Google share; they punch in and out of work with a mobile app on their cell phone, and to remain employed they must be advancing toward their GED.

Harlem Grown now has an annual budget of $1.5 million (Tony doesn't take a salary). Its first year it produced forty pounds of fresh produce; now it produces 5,400 pounds a year. It also composts, uses rainwater for drip irrigation, and even raises chickens. At fund-raisers, former students take the stage and describe how "Mr. Tony" taught them how to create healthy soil, gave them confidence in school, and inspired them to follow their dreams.

Tony has inspired a lot of us. When Tony met Mari at Aetna's African American calendar event in St. Louis, they were soon joined by other urban farmers, and together they went into a corner and developed a plan to build a blueprint for urban farms. That blueprint led to the Aetna Foundation's creation of 3,358 urban farms across America.

As Tony would tell you, it's not just about the farms. It's about showing up, getting your hands dirty, and changing people's lives. Mari and I had Tony and his staff to our house and spent a day developing a new operating plan, and we invited Harlem Grown's top fifty donors for dinner. When Mari was taking classes at Columbia University for her master's degree in occupational therapy, she brought her classmates to the farm and got them involved. When Mari graduated, her class donated a check to Harlem Grown, and even with Mari gone, Columbia students continue to work at the farm.

There are so many lessons here. Neither the city of New York nor the state of New York could have created Harlem Grown, and Lord knows, the federal government could not have, either. Only someone in the community could have done it. While Tony's life is, shall we say, more cinematic than most, there are people like Tony in every city and every town in America: leaders who understand their locale, who are invested in it, and who want to make it better. They just need our support.

In their charitable and philanthropic work, corporate leaders often talk about their desire to alleviate poverty and hunger, hardship and hopelessness, and I believe most of these leaders are sincere. But even those who try to understand these issues don't truly comprehend them unless they are on the ground and experiencing them—and my authority on this is Tony Hillery. As an African American who was once homeless, as a high school dropout who is a recovering alcoholic, he thought he understood these children and what their lives were like. But he didn't.

"This experience gave me a snapshot into a world that I knew but didn't know," he said. "You see it, but you don't see it. You hear it, but you don't hear it. You read about it, but you turn the page and don't remember it. Even videos—you watch it, it hits you, but you can't grasp it, and you watch another video. I was guilty of all that."

But no more. He planted a seed and watched it grow.

Hands in the soil are a gift to the soul.

Epilogue

LEGACY OF THE APOSTLES

IN 2013, I WAS INVITED TO THE WHITE HOUSE, ALONG with other CEOs, to meet with President Obama, who had just won reelection. He went around the table seeking our views on the budget, and various chief executives—Ginni Rometty at IBM, Jamie Dimon at JPMorgan Chase, Rex Tillerson at ExxonMobil—spoke up. I was the only one who had never met Obama, and when it was my turn, the president said, "You're the new guy. What do you think?"

Sitting next to me was Ford CEO Alan Mulally and, pointing to him, I said, "I used to work on this guy's assembly line. I went back to school so I could be a union steward, and now I'm running a Fortune 100 company."

"That's not bad," the president said.

I shared a few more details about my story (though I may have skipped that it took me eight years to earn my undergraduate degree), and I concluded, "I've lived the American Dream." I wanted to connect that idea to a specific policy, so I said: "Words matter. If you talk about 'entitlement reform,' those are the wrong words. It means that people are entitled. It should be, 'How do we make sure there is a safety net for everyone who wants to achieve the American Dream?'"

I told the president that after all the polarizing rhetoric of the campaign, we need to change the dialogue to something that is more unifying and aspirational. Why not explicitly invoke the American Dream? "If you ask me to help pay for that, then I've got an open checkbook. How much do you want? Because I want that for everybody."

When the other executives nodded, I assumed I struck the right chord. Obama turned and said, "You should be working for me."

"Mr. President," I joked, "you can't afford me."

He smiled and said, "You're a dollar-a-year kind of guy."

My living the American Dream is something that I never take for granted. With the help of family, friends, and colleagues, I have far exceeded anything that I thought imaginable, and that's why no one should mistake me for a pessimist. While this book has described some of the challenges in our workplaces and in society, I also believe that young people have far more opportunities than ever before.

When I talk to college students, I tell them, first, that their university would have never accepted me when I was applying to undergraduate programs, and it probably wouldn't have accepted me for graduate school, either. I didn't have the grades, didn't have the scores, and with my long hair, blue jeans, and sandals, I didn't have the look. So, it's not about where you start in life. It's about the journey, and what direction you are headed, and whether you have the determination and character to reach your goals.

Next, I tell the students that they think they are living through tough times, but when I was growing up, we had the Vietnam War, urban riots, campus protests, and widespread disillusionment with our institutions and leaders. Young men coming home in body bags? *Those* were tough times, and they were more challenging in other ways. Our pathways to success—for the most part, a job in corporate America—were

clearly defined but also limited. Now our broadband era has shattered the old corporate models and has created unprecedented opportunity. You can invent what you want to invent, live where you want to live, and sell your products or services to customers all over the world. More than any time in our history, you can be who you want to be.

Finally, I offer the students the following advice:

Do something that you do well and love to do.

Always know where you need to be.

Use a moral compass that tells you how to behave.

And what other people think of you is none of your business.

AS A GRANDPARENT, I believe I'm even more mindful of the future, and I recognize how blessed I've been with my own children.

Eric is now thirty-two, and what strikes me is the utter normalcy of his life. He lives in a small town in New Hampshire with his wife, Lee, and their beautiful daughter, Kayley. He takes her to the park. He has an exercise machine in the basement. He's studying for his doctorate so he can teach. He and Lee are talking about a second child. I see that he's happy, and I know that if I were in my thirties, that's the life that would make me happy. What better way to make a difference than teaching? What better way to live than to be part of a close-knit community? I chose a different route. I did so in part out of financial necessity, and I also knew that I had certain business skills. We all choose our own path, and I look at Eric's with both admiration and pride.

If Eric reminds me of the life that I might have had, Lauren reminds me of the life that I have had. She is now thirty, living in Brooklyn with her husband, Sam, and she has a thriving career in Internet media. After Gawker filed for Chapter 11, Univision acquired its sprawling online assets, renamed the business, and soon named Lauren its chief operating officer, an immense responsibility for someone so young. We'd often share long dinners, longer walks, and many conversations about the corporate world.

One night she asked me, "Dad, when does it get easier?"

"What do you mean?"

"When the business is running fine and you can go home and spend the weekend with your family?"

"If you're going to drive change," I said, "buckle in, because it never gets easier."

In 2017, Lauren was hired by *The Daily Beast* to be its chief product officer; she now sits in meetings with Barry Diller, who is chairman of IAC, the holding company that owns *The Daily Beast*.

Lauren called me. "How do I deal with Barry Diller?" she asked.

"First thing," I said, "you call him Mr. Diller. And then as soon as you tell him what you're going to do, he's going to demand that it be done shorter and cheaper and generate bigger results."

A week later, she called me back and said, "That's what happened! How did you know that?"

"Because that's what I do!"

On another occasion, we were supposed to leave town one weekend for a brief getaway, but she had late meetings and asked if we could delay our departure because she was too busy.

Yes, I said, I know what that's like. And the moment re-minded me of Harry Chapin's wistful ballad "Cat's in the Cradle." My girl was just like me. I just hope she's happy.

Mari was formerly my cranialsacral therapist and yoga instructor, then later became my partner. In 2018, she be-came my wife. She said she always wanted to be married but didn't want to get married, so we eloped, flying to Taos, New Mexico, with our new dog, Keeva, a sable German shepherd. We said our vows in the Sangre de Cristo Mountains. Mari wore a white dress and cowboy boots. I wore a tux with my cowboy boots. Keeva was the ring bearer. Our officiant was a minister; her daughter and her boyfriend were our witnesses, with the daughter doubling as our photographer.

Mari works in schools in Harlem, teaching kids how to read, and she sits on the boards of Harlem Grown and Brooklyn to Alaska, a nonprofit that brings urban youth to the wilderness of our forty-ninth state. She is also heavily in-volved in our Anahata Foundation, and if it is properly man-aged, it will last another hundred years to support community and rural development. As Mari likes to say, "We don't have our own kids, but we're creating different kinds of things."

Any talk of legacy brings to mind my visit to the famous Church of Santa Croce in Florence, the world's largest Fran-ciscan church and the burial place for Michelangelo, Ma-chiavelli, Galileo, Foscolo, and Rossini. With their tombs embedded in the walls (and there is an empty tomb for Dante), the church is known as "the Temple of the Italian Glories." None of these men died wealthy, but their contributions were so immense—in art, literature, music, and philosophy—that wealthy Italians paid to be buried in the floor of the church. Money allowed them proximity to greatness, even in death.

Then, in 1966, the Arno River breached its levees in a Florence suburb, and the authorities, fearing that two over-loaded dams would collapse, discharged more than 10 million tons of water into the city. The deluge claimed more than 100 lives and left 20,000 homeless while damaging many of the city's architectural and cultural landmarks. The flood also dumped almost nine feet of water, oil, and mud into the Church of Santa Croce, defacing many of its paintings, mosaics, and altarpieces. According to my tour guide, the torrent also washed away the remains of the wealthy Italians who had paid to be buried there. The tombs of the artists, writers, and composers, however, survived the onslaught and remain in the church to this day.

The metaphor speaks volumes. You cannot buy immortality, and what you purchase, including burial plots, is forever exposed and vulnerable. If you want to survive the ages, think about what really matters. Art. Music. Literature. The contours of beauty in all its forms. Think about the "Italian glories," who continue to inspire and awe, their tombs intact, their creations honored, their names venerated. Wealth should be used for impact and change, not for expressions of vanity.

I am sometimes asked about my legacy. I won't be putting my name on any buildings or monuments, all of which could be washed away in the next storm. And I don't have the gifts of a Renaissance painter or sculptor. But I still hope to leave something of value, what I call "the legacy of the apostles."

In the Bible, the twelve apostles were the followers of Jesus who carried his message of love and compassion into the world. When you think about it, that act of communication, that spreading of ideas, is what all leaders in all walks of life try to do.

We strive to communicate what we know so that others can embrace those messages and teach them to others. That is perhaps the most difficult challenge for every large organization, including those that I led. I would tell my senior leaders what has to happen, and they would tell their leaders, but by the time my message reached the front lines, it often bore little resemblance to what I said originally. That was on me, the leader, to find a better way of communicating the message.

And it remains on me. I don't want to be remembered for anything that I achieved. I want to be remembered for what I've taught, because those lessons—I hope—will be passed on, enhanced, and amplified by those who have been part of my life. That legacy doesn't have a name, a banner, or a website, but I'd like to consider it the legacy of the apostles.

IT'S BEEN FOURTEEN YEARS since my spinal cord injury, and my arm still flares with pain when the barometric pressure drops. But most people who meet me don't even know that I have the injury, and I remain determined to live a full and productive life. That means bike rides down Sixth Avenue, hiking mountain ranges around the country, and motorcycling around New England and across the United States. I know that I am creating even more stress on my joints and limbs, and I can feel their diminishment . . . but that's okay. If you tell me that I can continue to do the things that I enjoy doing even if it means a shorter life, I'll take that deal.

I don't mind challenges, and I already faced the one that I most feared.

Vermont has a program, called Adaptive Ski and Sports, that helps disabled athletes, and it operates at several sites, including Killington. I could have gone to another mountain, but as I was approaching the two-year anniversary of my injury, I knew I had to go back to *the* mountain and *the* run. I was so nervous on the drive up, I had to fight the impulse to turn around.

But I arrived, and I walked into the lodge with skis, boots, and poles, and I told the instructor for the Adaptive program what had happened.

"Okay," Joe said, "leave your poles here, and let's go to the magic carpet."

Out we went, and the sliding carpet gently carried me up the Bunny Hill.

"Ski down to the bottom!" Joe yelled.

So, I did, without hesitation or trouble.

"You used to race," Joe said.

"Yeah."

"You're a really good skier."

"Yeah."

"So, what are we doing here? Let's go up."

We took a lift on an intermediate slope. I could no longer use poles, so Joe gave me a lanyard to put around my neck and told me to hold it with my left hand. We worked on positioning my body over the skis and how to turn without the usual movement of my arms or the benefit of poles. I was afraid and had real doubts. But I knew what the correct weight distribution was over the skis, and I knew that my legs had to do all the work and that my upper body had to be still and always square to the fall line. So exactly two years after my accident, in the exact same conditions—bright sun, warm day—I pushed off and headed down the hill.

I was tentative that first run, and not much better the second time down. But by the third run, I was more confident, and faster, and it was effortless, almost like a dream . . . the grooves in the snow . . . the wind in my face . . . the hell-bent speed . . . and I felt that oneness with the mountain. The adrenaline surged, and the tears fell. *Oh my God. I can ski!*

When I came to a stop, Joe said, "Let's do the run where you fell."

We took the lift, reached the top, and were off again. I knew where the tree was. I had actually hiked up earlier—it took forty-five minutes—because I wanted to see it, to touch it. Now, heading down Bear Mountain, I saw it in the distance, glided over, and came to a stop.

The instructor waited patiently.

The real emotion came as I flew down the trails, proving I could do what I thought I could never do again. Now as I faced that tree, it was a very quiet, very still moment. I felt not so much triumphant as defiant.

This is where it had ended the last time, but it was not going to end here this time.

I pushed off, leaned forward, and sped down the hill.

My journey was just beginning.

Acknowledgments

THE ACT OF WRITING A BOOK IS ALWAYS A JOURNEY WITH many able and insightful people holding your hand while keeping you to a schedule! While these acknowledgments will miss a few people who have made this book possible, I deeply appreciate all those who by example or in face-to-face feedback shaped me as an executive. I often comment that my leadership style is a mosaic of the good and bad behaviors I have assimilated along my journey through life. It is that mosaic that has created the story you are about to read.

To my parents and family of sisters, brothers, cousins, aunts, uncles, and grandparents, you have made my life a rich and wonderful journey. To my many mentors, bosses, and leadership teams throughout my career, your feedback has been invaluable. I know I didn't always express my appreciation gracefully! To many of my teachers and professors, your patience has shaped my heuristic about the world and has allowed me to frame my work purposefully. To my close friends who walked the same streets, went to the same schools, attended the same parties, and always took care of me when the chips were down, I promise you that one day you will recover from the shock of my success!

To my good friend and colleague Steve Kelmar, your insights, prodding and insistence on excellence has made me a better leader and this book a reality. Along with David Aveni, your patience in reviewing and commenting on the myriad drafts was invaluable!

The Currency team has made the work of publishing this book a lot easier for me at a very hectic time in my life. A big thanks to Currency's publisher, Tina Constable, and her deputy publisher, Campbell Wharton, to Hayley Shear in marketing, and publicist Steven Boriack. Currency's editor Roger Scholl has been invaluable in his feedback and encouragement. Last but not least, Erin Little, editorial assistant, made the wheels turn throughout the final push to printing.

A final bow of gratitude to Jim Hirsch. His patience, probing, and pushing kept this project moving ahead. He spent more time than I did in understanding the nuances in my journey. He found my voice in expressing that journey in an accessible way. Jim, my time with you was a privilege that shaped my heuristic more than you can know.

Index